DEADWOOD

The Best Writings on the Most Notorious Town in the West

Edited by T. D. Griffith

TWODOT®

GUILFORD, CONNECTICUT
HELENA, MONTANA
AN IMPRINT OF THE GLOBE PEQUOT PRESS

A · **T W O D O T**® · **B O O K**

Copyright © 2010 by Morris Book Publishing, LLC

TwoDot is a registered trademark of Morris Book Publishing, LLC

Text design: Sheryl P. Kober
Project editor: Julie Marsh
Layout: Lisa Reneson

Library of Congress Cataloging-in-Publication Data
Deadwood : the best writings on the most notorious town in the West / edited by T. D. Griffith.
    p. cm.
  Includes index.
  ISBN 978-0-7627-5416-8
  1. Deadwood (S.D.)—History. 2. Frontier and pioneer life—South Dakota—Deadwood. I. Griffith,
T. D. (Tom D.), 1958-
  F659.D2D276 2010
  978.3'91—dc22

                                                                                    2009034231

Printed in the United States of America

10 9 8 7 6 5 4 3 2 1

For my sagacious siblings,
Mark, Mike, Jim, Patrick, & Lisa,
with whom I first explored the American West

CONTENTS

Preface: The Original Sin City viii
by T. D. Griffith

Acknowledgments xiii

PART I
THE MAIN STREET IS BOTTOMLESS

"Life in a Gold Rush Town" 3
Watson Parker
1966

"Deadwood in the Spring of 1877" 23
May 1877

A Brother's Letter 26
January 1878

"Doomed: The Rise & Fall of Deadwood's Chinatown" 29
Dustin D. Floyd
February 2006

"The Murder of Preacher Smith" 38
John S. McClintock
1939

"From Sin to Cinders" 50
Bob Lee, Stan Lindstrom, Wynn Lindstrom, Editors
1976

"Deadwood—A Modern Sodom Needs Another Renovation" . . . 72
Edward L. Senn
December 1938

PART II
WILD BILL HICKOCK AND CALAMITY JANE

"Wild Bill's Demise" 80
Joseph G. Rosa
1974

"Calamity Jane—With Wild Bill Hickok in Deadwood, 1876" . . . 88
James D. McLaird
2005

"Wild Bill Hickok and His Magic Touch" and "That's No Man—
That's Calamity Jane" 102
Helen Rezatto
1983

PART III
PIONEERS AND PERSONALITIES

"Firsts—Explorers, Cooks & Teachers" 121
Helen Rezatto
1983

"The Mystery Man," Tom Moore 134
Frank B. Bryant
Circa 1930 (?)

"A Little Girl in Deadwood" 140
Estelline Bennett
1928

"Madame Moustache and Poker Alice" 163
Michael Rutter
2005

"Like One Forsaken" 174
W. E. Adams
1925

Contents   v

PART IV
THE LEGEND CONTINUES

"The Color: Gold Makes a Man a Man and Lifts Us Up Above the Baboons". 177
David Milch
2006

"Deadwood Mountain" 184
Big Kenny, John Rich, Paul Worley
2004

"Haunted Spots" 187
Chad Lewis and Terry Fisk
2006

"We're All Out of Touch". 200
Pete Dexter
1986

Permissions and Acknowledgments 209
Index. 211
About the Editor. 215

Deadwood in 1877 was showing a hint of commerce, as commercial buildings and new residences began appearing, some perched precariously on the slopes of the pine-clad cliffs. (Photo courtesy of Adams Museum, Deadwood, SD)

PREFACE:
THE ORIGINAL SIN CITY

Though others have laid claim, Deadwood was the West's original sin city. Just weeks after the cry of "gold" echoed through the pine-clad coulees, the blood began pouring as freely as the beer and whiskey. Sultry upstairs girls used their wiles to winnow away the gold dust of played-out prospectors. Faro tables and mining supplies usually consumed the rest. Gun shots were not that unusual, nor was death due to other than natural causes.

There was a time when it wasn't safe to walk these brick-lined streets, though that was a dozen gunfights, barroom brawls, and a century ago. At times wicked, ribald, and reviled, today's Deadwood retains some of that swagger and a bit of the smart-ass smirk that distinguished it from so many other gold camps of the West.

This is the town that witnessed Wild Bill Hickok gunned down while playing poker with his back to the door. These are the same streets that felt the footprints and heard the coyote-howl of Calamity Jane Canary, the one-woman cyclone who claimed she could out-drink, out-swear, and out-spit *any* man. And, Lord, how she tried.

Initially constructed in a ramshackle way, a succession of floods and fires forced a more uniform approach to urban planning in a place confined by steep-sided canyons. Prior to the turn of the twen-tieth century, much of the city's new-found wealth wound its way into the pockets of merchants, bankers, and saloon-keepers who cleverly invested it in beautiful Victorian buildings and residences that today stand as testament to a richer, yet rougher time. Before it was civi-lized, Deadwood was anything but a haven for the well-heeled, the well-mannered, and the righteous.

After a few centuries of sporadic visits from nomadic Plains Indian tribes, in 1874 Lt. Col. George Armstrong Custer led one hundred wagons and 1,000 men into the Black Hills of Dakota Territory—the last remaining uncharted region of the United States. Western settlement had previously bypassed the ancient mountain range, due to the federal government's treaty with the Lakota Sioux tribe that had created the Great Sioux Reservation. Ordered to map the emerald oasis of the Black Hills in 1874, Custer and his assemblage of soldiers, newspaper reporters, photographers, cartographers, and geologists also confirmed the presence of gold and news of the "strike" was quickly dispatched to Eastern newspapers. The reports set in motion a wave of miners, muleskinners, and madams who sailed their prairie schooners and freight wagons across the vast sea of prairie known as the Great Plains to the unknown frontier of Paha Sapa (in Lakota, literally "hills black").

The U.S. Army briefly attempted to honor its treaty with Native Americans, escorting the would-be miners and settlers out of the Black Hills at gunpoint to military forts in nearby states. But the effort proved futile, as the cascade of gold-seekers swelled to unmanageable levels. In a matter of months, Deadwood bulged from a few ramshackle huts to more than 7,000 uninvited residents. By 1876, an estimated 10,000 fortune-hunters had set up permanent camp in the area of Deadwood Gulch, where lawlessness and primitive conditions contributed to what some historians have described as a death a day.

Sporadic gunfights and misdirected gunfire certainly contributed to the more unremarkable forms of untimely demise, but settlers in this new frontier also had to be concerned with consumption, freezing, fever, and pneumonia, among the most common causes of death in the early years. As the town grew, so did the list of reasons for taking the proverbial dirt nap, adding gravel, worms, alcoholism, heart disease, sunstroke, and teething, as well as getting struck by lightning, killed by Indians, kicked by a horse, murdered, gored, scalded, struck by a falling body, and "shot sparking another man's wife."

Yes, it took time for civilization to take root in the fabled Black Hills, where life was cheap and claim disputes were often settled with six-guns. But, without that adolescent period of recklessness, Deadwood wouldn't have been much of a story today, let alone cause for a book or an original HBO series.

Through fire and flood, boom and bust, then boom again, the legend of Deadwood continues. When Deadwood sprang to life in the gulch in 1876, businesses, banks, and homes were constructed of wood. But the town's first decade witnessed entire areas of downtown destroyed by successive fires and floods. Tired of the labor and expense of rebuilding time and again, successful merchants and bankers began constructing their new buildings in native stone. More than one hundred years later, those Victorian buildings with elaborate facades still stand in downtown Deadwood as testament to the wealth that lay beneath its soil.

-1881-
Calamity
Jane.
Age- 29 yrs.
x   Calamity Jane
Died Aug. 1-1903 and buried beside
"Wild Bill" at Deadwood - So. Dak.

All dressed up, Calamity Jane at age twenty-nine in 1881, strikes a studio pose. She lived an unusual life of fame, poverty, and prostitution, before being buried beside Wild Bill Hickok in Deadwood in 1903.

(Photo courtesy of Adams Museum, Deadwood, SD)

From its rough and tumble beginnings as a frontier town, gold dust fueled a transformation. That changed a hodge-podge of quickly constructed shacks and sheds to a civilized community featuring theaters, churches, and Sunday afternoon socials. The first telephone lines were installed in 1879, just three years after the first miners stumbled into the gulch and only a year after the first tele-

The buzz of saws and the sound of hammers pounding could be heard on Deadwood's Main Street in June 1876, as new buildings sprang from the ground and the dull roar of saloons and gambling halls disquieted the night. Prospectors lived in tents and shanties until more suitable accommodations were constructed. (Photo courtesy of Adams Museum, Deadwood, SD)

phone had been installed in the White House. In 1883 electric lights began illuminating the homes, businesses, and streets of Deadwood, long before such conveniences followed the plow across the prairie to the average farming community.

For the next century, Deadwood followed a familiar pattern of highs and lows that generally echoed the nation's economy and, specifically, the price of gold. But in the 1980s, with corporate mining in decline, Deadwood was nearly dead. Historic preservation officials who were witnessing the slow deterioration of the town's once-proud past labeled it "a disaster." Streets were decaying, building facades were crumbling, and, except for the few summer months when families flocked to the Black Hills and nearby Mount Rushmore National Memorial, employment opportunities were wanting.

After a century of boom-bust cycles, Deadwood was just a remnant of its glorious past. Vacant commercial buildings and declining employment opportunities for the town's younger residents sent a signal of despair. What remained was a storied past filled with colorful characters who helped shape the West, vacant buildings with once-proud Victorian facades, and a dubious future.

Unwilling to forfeit one of South Dakota's cultural and historic treasures, voters in 1989 approved limited-stakes gaming to generate revenues that would then be dedicated to restoring and preserving this mile-high community. That fall, Deadwood launched a revolutionary experiment in economic development and historic preservation by becoming just the third venue in the United States (behind the state of Nevada and Atlantic City, New Jersey) to offer legalized gambling. Two decades, 2,500 new jobs, and $200 million in historic improvement projects later, most people call it a success.

Brick streets, period lighting, and colorful trolleys greet visitors who spend hours testing their luck in the town's eighty gaming halls, taking historic walking tours, visiting Wild Bill and Calamity Jane at Mt. Moriah Cemetery, and exploring historic homes and the Adams Museum. A regular slate of rodeos, vintage car shows, Wild West re-enactments, St. Patrick's Day and Mardi Gras celebrations, and free Main Street concerts keeps visitors and locals entertained throughout the year.

Today, the community of only 1,380 residents welcomes nearly two million yearly visitors and is one of only a handful in America designated a National Historic Landmark. This is Deadwood, the town that decided to save itself.

—*T. D. Griffith*

ACKNOWLEDGMENTS

Any topic that involves "best" is purely subjective and open to continuing debate. But, when The Globe Pequot Press announced its intent to publish this work, *Deadwood: The Best Writings on the Most Notorious Town in the West,* as the third in its series, I nearly fell off my horse reaching for my Blackberry. It wasn't due to any prospective byline, but rather the passion I feel for my adopted home of Deadwood, where a cast of characters as colorful and engaging as any in the Old West still resides.

In selecting entries for the best writing about Deadwood, it was my intent to tell something of the town's evolution through the voices of those who actually came here. Various mediums that engage the written word should be represented, I surmised, including literary extracts from noted scholars, dramatic treatments from distinguished novelists, and popular songs from contemporary performers. But, so too should the common man's recollection be incorporated, lest we forget those who toiled in sweat with shovel and sluice and six-gun to tame this often god-forsaken place. Consequently, the reader will wonder at the near-illiterate letter of a tired prospector to his family back home and the diary entry of a prominent Deadwood entrepreneur written in his deepest despair.

None of these remarkable accounts would have been combined for a book by me without the gentle guidance and direction of Deadwood history-lovers such as Adams Museum director Mary Kopco and her equally enthusiastic staff: Jerry Bryant, Rose Speirs, Arlette Hanson, and Darrell Nelson. Thanks as well to Janelle Moody-Chaney of the Deadwood Public Library. Each has my deepest appreciation for sharing insights and recommendations from the diverse collections of these two fine institutions.

Also to be acknowledged are my friends, authors Joseph Rosa and Pete Dexter, and country singer/songwriters Big Kenny Alphin and John Rich, whose collective successes provide a window not only to the

Prospectors who have just purchased supplies at the Big Horn Store in 1876 ready their wares for the trek to their claims. (Photo courtesy of Adams Museum, Deadwood, SD)

Wild West, but to the strengths and weaknesses of the human soul. Thanks, too, to ally Shawn Pennington of Nashville, who helped me navigate the intricacies of music licensing on the Left and Right Coasts, to Deadwood Historic Preservation officer Kevin Kuchenbecker, and to my Globe Pequot editors, Erin Turner and Allen Jones, who suffered my innumerable queries with patience and poise.

In just a matter of weeks in the summer of 1876, as many as 10,000 miners descended on the gold-filled gulch of Deadwood and began building their collective future. (Photo courtesy of Adams Museum, Deadwood, SD)

Finally, my fondest appreciation is extended to my wife, Nyla Griffith, a fellow writer and one of my few friends who understand that solitary pursuit and expression can often lead to the next grand adventure.

James Butler "Wild Bill" Hickok in buckskins, as he may have appeared to miners upon arrival in Deadwood in the summer of 1876. (Photo courtesy of Adams Museum, Deadwood, SD)

PART I

THE MAIN STREET
IS BOTTOMLESS

Early-day life in Deadwood was everything but easy. If you were a prospector, bare-knuckling your future knee-deep in a cold creek with a gold pan and an eye for some color, you started in a tent if you were lucky, then moved up to a ramshackle structure nailed together with whatever downed timber you could scavenge. If you had a stake, you shared a room with other itinerant miners of varied dispositions in a local boardinghouse. Some of these fortune-seekers struck it rich. Others moved on to richer strikes. Still some took sick, while others died.

Nearby communities, many now just long-forgotten ghost towns, were established in 1876 wherever miners hoarded gold dust. The following spring, the *Chicago Times* reported that the entire ancient mountain range of the Black Hills, an area roughly the size of Delaware, had a population of 15,250. Rapid City, today the largest community in western South Dakota, had just 250 residents; Crook City claimed 400; and Troy, briefly known as Gayville, and the upper portions of the gulch, boasted another 3,000 inhabitants.

By May 1877, just eight months after Wild Bill Hickok bled out after an ill-fated poker game in Deadwood, farmers were already tilling the flatlands and running cattle in waist-high grass. Someone, the *Times* noted, had to feed all these miners, muleskinners, and madams. "The success of the mining interests of the Black Hills is now fairly assured," the reporter wrote, "and farmers may therefore hope for good markets. There is much good land still unoccupied and the farming business is not likely to be overdone for another year or two."

In the midst of this newfound El Dorado, newcomers squatted wherever there was room and ate virtually anything they could find. "Hotels charge two to four dollars per day. Common price at restaurants has been a ticket for twenty-one meals for ten dollars, the ticket-holder having the privilege of sleeping on his own blankets on the ground floor of the palatial establishment," the *Times* told its readers. "Miners frequently get boarded for $8 to $10 per week, while they often club together and board themselves for even less."

Just three years removed from even being mapped, the Black Hills was America's great new frontier. Its mystique, amplified by the fodder of so many dime store novels and unabashedly optimistic Eastern newspaper accounts, attracted the notable and the unknown. Gunfighters, gamblers, and sultry upstairs girls added to the legend, the lure, and the lore. In a place far from civilization and the long arm of the law, where distrust for authority was accompanied by sidearms, long rifles, and sharp knives, gold dust was the currency of choice. With it came comfort, accommodation and a lust for more. Without it, life could indeed be a long and lonely road.

"Gold dust is the money of the Black Hills, and it is reckoned at $20 to the ounce, making the pennyweight equal to a dollar, and six grains equal to a quarter, which is the lowest denomination in practical use," the *Times* said. "The real value of Deadwood gold is about $18 currency to the ounce, and therefore prices are 11 percent higher than the actual fact. People going into the Hills get their greenbacks changed for gold dust at one of the banks before making many small purchases. The gold of the other creeks is generally more valuable than that of Deadwood, but none comes fully up to the nominal price of $20."

"LIFE IN A GOLD RUSH TOWN"
FROM *GOLD IN THE BLACK HILLS*
WATSON PARKER
1966

The product of a Black Hills dude ranch, noted historian Watson Parker earned his doctorate in Western American history from the University of Oklahoma in 1965 and penned Gold in the Black Hills *the following year. He spent his career teaching at the University of Wisconsin–Oshkosh, tending to the ancestral ranch near Hill City, researching Black Hills history, and becoming one of the region's most prolific authors.*

"Life in a Gold Rush Town," taken from Gold in the Black Hills, *provides what might be regarded as the definitive historical account of life the way it really was in the early years of Deadwood Gulch—hard work coupled with bad whiskey, bad breath, bad winters, mud that stuck to everything and everybody, hot baths, cold baths, dry vapor, sulphur, alcohol, and shower baths, all accompanied by the constant smell of wood smoke and the bone-chilling howl of Smokey Jones.*

Methodically researched, comprehensive, and simply presented, Parker's work is generally regarded as the authority in its field. As the Journal of American History *said of the work, "Every aspect of the rush is presented: the early propaganda that inspired it, the actual movement of population to that isolated clump of mountains in western South Dakota, relations with the Indians, early mining methods, social and political connections, and bandits and frontier justice."*

Put away his pick and shovel,
He will never prospect more;
Death has sluiced him from his trouble,
Panned him on the other shore.

The tale of the men who came to the Hills, of the way they lived, and of the amusements with which they whiled away their idle hours is a fascinating one. Obviously, it is easier to read their story now than it was to live it then, but, all things considered, it was a rewarding experience.

The first-comers were men, for few women and no "ladies" joined the rush to the early placer mines. Even Mrs. R. B. Fay, who arrived on the first coach to Deadwood, was referred to as "the first lady passenger," a compliment which seems rather thoughtless inasmuch as there already was a well-patronized millinery shop in town. Nor were there many children in the Hills in comparison to the total population, judging by the small number attending the various schools.

Photographs taken during the gold rush show bearded miners in profusion, and the first impression is that the rushers were older men. A closer look, however, reveals youthful eyes behind the whiskers, and well it might: the median age in Deadwood was thirty, five years less than that of the adult population in the United States at the time. The following table, derived from the roster of the Society of Black Hills Pioneers, tells the story:

POPULATION OF THE BLACK HILLS, 1875

Age	Percent
Under 20	10
Between 21 and 30	43
Between 31 and 40	35
Between 41 and 50	10
Over 50	2
Total	100

Most of these men came from the East; nearly two-fifths were born in New York, Pennsylvania, Ohio, Illinois, and Kentucky. Another two-fifths were born in foreign countries, a proportion which far exceeded even that of the West as a whole where only 25 percent of the population in 1870 was foreign-born. Of course, many

The prospect of gold led fortune-hunters to descend on the Black Hills in 1876. Muleskinners, madams, and merchants soon followed the "color."

(Photo courtesy of the Adams Museum, Deadwood, SD)

who came to the Hills had originally joined gold rushes to California, Nevada, Colorado, and Montana, but then turned eastward when the new Dakota mines were discovered. Two other groups were prominent in the rush: the Chinese and the Negroes. The former came to Deadwood in sufficient numbers to form their own Chinatown in the heart of the city, from which incense wafted over the whole gulch. The latter, although less cohesive, staged at least one large picnic, on August 2, 1879, in honor of the freedom earlier achieved by their race in Santo Domingo.

This heterogeneous aggregation soon developed a unifying spirit of co-operation and mutual responsibility. A few prospectors were secretive and suspicious, keeping all knowledge of new discoveries to themselves. Most, however, shared good news and anything else they had, even with total strangers. The campfire was free to everyone, for the miners understood that in a new land hospitality was a virtue upon which all might one day need to call. In addition, strangers brought news and made good company for isolated miners tired of faithful friends and faces. At any rate, the generous hospitality of the miner was proverbial. To be on hand at mealtime assured an invitation, and to arrive in camp at dusk always meant that there would be a place to sleep in the tent or cabin.

POPULATION OF BLACK HILLS BY PLACE OF BIRTH

	Percent		Percent
New York	14	British Isles	18
Pennsylvania	8	Germany-Prussia	13
Ohio	7	Canada	5
Illinois	6	All other foreign	6
Kentucky	4	------	
Total, 5 states	39	Total, foreign born	42
All other states	19	Total U.S.	58
Total, U.S. born	58	Total	100

The miners' friendliness is generally said to have been equaled by their honesty, but the latter virtue was represented more by tradition than by the actual conditions. Nevertheless, custom dictated that a miner's claim, his tools, and his gold were inviolable, as safe when he went to town as if he had remained to watch them. Furthermore, most of the miners were well armed and did not hesitate to shoot in defense of their property. In the early days of the rush personal law enforcement probably prevented many petty crimes. Unfortunately, as the rush progressed, the prospectors were joined by camp followers who would pick up anything not solidly attached to bedrock. "Not even a bucket, brush, broom, strap, halter, or, in fact, any small article," grumbled the *Black Hills Pioneer,* was safe outside after dark. One woman complained that a thief had removed three joints of pipe from her stove and would have taken the stove, too, if it had not been too hot to handle. These petty crimes increased as the early community spirit of the placers gave way to the more business-like attitude of the hard-rock miners. Nevertheless, a tradition of "frontier honesty" persisted until the railroads came in the 1880's, even though the prudent did not rely upon it very heavily.

Isolated male groups doing essentially the same work tend to develop their own slang and their own catchwords, remarks which by continued use are accepted as meaningful in the most unexpected contexts. Such a phrase was "Whoa, Emma!" It was vague enough to be available for general use and yet capable of inflections suited to every need. The uninitiated may have supposed it to be somehow connected with the "Emma Mine" swindle, and thus both topical and appropriate during a mining boom. Actually it seems to have been derived from the lines "0 day, the fairest one that ever rose,/ Period and end of anxious Emma's woes," by the seventeenth-century English poet Matthew Prior.

Another common phrase of Deadwood Gulch was the cry "Oh, Joe!" which would start after supper at the head of the valley and work its way from tent to tent. It gathered volume as additional voices swelled the chorus, until it echoed away in the rocks and rubble beyond the farthest camp. The call was said to have originated in the piteous cries of a drunken prospector who fell into a hole one evening and spent the night fruitlessly bellowing for assistance.

To lugubrious calls for "Joe" was often added the plaintive, penetrating lone-wolf howl of Smokey Jones. His was a sound calculated to raise the hackles, chill the blood, and undo the resolution of even the bravest miner. It was dearly loved by all. Jones one day made his pile in the mines and departed for the East. Several months later he came back again, a shaved and polished stranger who passed unrecognized amongst his dearest friends until one night at the Gem Theater where he joined in the applause by giving his old, familiar howl. Great was the miners' rejoicing—Smokey Jones was back again!

An aspect of Western talk which strangers found amusing was the indiscriminate bestowal of military and judicial titles. Among 1,500 names in the Pierre directory, for example, there were 800 colonels, approximately 200 majors and judges, and a liberal sprinkling of captains. "Professor," however, seems to have been reserved for school and music teachers and men who "played piano" in theaters and bars.

When introduced to one of these titled luminaries, the proper salutation was always, "Howdy." If a new acquaintance proved a good fellow, one said he was "a white man, yes sir," with heavy emphasis on the final word. If he possessed learning, he was said to be a "sharp," as in "rock sharp" for an assayer or geologist, or "gospel sharp" for a minister. When death dissolved a friendship, the departed was said to have "gone up the flume." An epitaph like the one at the beginning of this chapter might be rudely hand-carved on a headboard, and pious hopes expressed that everything would "pan out all right" for him in "the big diggings up the crick."

Room and board offered a staple topic for conversation or doggerel:

> *The beefsteak is of leather,*
> *And the pies are made of tin;*
> *The bread you could not cut it with a sword,*
> *The butter wears side-whiskers,*
> *The coffee's very thin,*
> *In the little, one-horse hash-house where I board.*

The best quality board cost as much as $14 a week, but thrift miners "batching" in a mess of five or six could eat for half that amount if they could stand their own cooking. Flour cost about $10 for one hundred pounds (although it once soared to $60 during a winter shortage), bacon approximately twenty-five cents a pound, butter, forty cents, eggs, thirty-five cents or more per dozen, depending upon supply. Two- and three-room cabins rented for $25 to $40 a month—but many men built their own of logs, brush, and canvas. An astonishing decorative feature was the brightly printed calico that the miners used for wallpaper. It fitted nicely over the rough logs and gave the cabins a cheerful look. George Stokes sold thousands of yards of it from his clothing store in Deadwood and astonished his wholesaler, who wondered how so few women could use so much cloth.

The first hotel in Deadwood was Charles H. Wagner's Grand Central. Here a traveler could get a rude bunk or space on the floor for his blankets at $1.00 a night. Wagner's board, fortunately, was much better than his beds for he had secured the services of "Aunt Lou" Marshbanks, a highly talented colored woman, and his table was justly famous. As the hotels improved, prices rose from $2.00 to $4.00 a day. Ordinary dining rooms and restaurants issued tickets good for a week's fare for about $10. Such places also acted as hotels, for the "meal tickets" often included the dubious privilege of sleeping on the floor of the establishment.

The comfort of a warm meal and a dry bed were especially appreciated during the gold rush, for the weather then was colder and wetter than at present. November, 1876, saw a heavy snow, and the editor of the *Cheyenne Daily Leader* mentioned that he was able to heat his office by burning the manuscripts he received from local poets about the "snow, beautiful snow." In October, 1877, Deadwood had a two-foot snowfall. The following spring a memorable five-day storm left seven feet of "the beautiful," as it was called, on the ground. Many roofs collapsed, and not surprisingly, for a platform scale used to weigh hay wagons registered 3,165 pounds of snow. When winds came up at the end of the storm, the snow was whipped into twenty-foot drifts, which later melted and resulted in severe flooding. The next month a second flood, caused by four days of steady rain, washed out placer workings, ruined roads, and filled up mines. A week later the weather turned cold again, and nearby Rapid City was blanketed with still another three feet of snow. Often these storms were followed by a chinook, a warm, southerly wind which could raise subzero temperatures fifty degrees in an hour or two and turn the ice to slush and mud.

Deadwood mud, moreover, was not ordinary mud, but "of a rich quality, its adhesive properties rare, its depth unfathomable, its color indefinable, its extent illimitable, and its usefulness unknown." Six and eight mules to the wagon could scarcely navigate through this Stygian liquid, which daubed the animals to their ears and completely disguised their color. Pedestrians waded through the tenacious muck and bellowed long, generous, liberal curses at the teamsters who had splashed them, the roadside buildings which blocked the drainage, and the fate which had brought them all to Deadwood. The streets continued in liquid condition most of the year for winter snows gave way to spring and summer rains. The local habit of throwing garbage into the street and the contributions made by passing livestock did little to make the slime more attractive.

The stinking mud and general lack of sanitation attracted swarms of flies. These, however, were common everywhere and were usually ignored. Lice, on the other hand, received more attention, for miners considered their presence a disgrace. One bullwhacker said that he had been plagued continuously by these pests for six years and still had not got used to them. Most of the men were more fastidious and boiled their clothes, applied "blue ointment" (Unguentum Hydrargyri), and tried to keep their shanties clean. One of the main exceptions to frontier hospitality was the hostility shown the lousy visitor, though usually his condition did not become apparent until the damage had been done.

The miner who found himself afflicted with lice or, indeed, almost any disease could resort to the Deadwood Bath House. This establishment advertised "hot baths, cold baths, dry vapor, sulphur, alcohol, and shower baths," and in smaller type discreetly mentioned "private disease, sure cure or no pay." One wonders what heroic treatments made possible such a guarantee.

If the bathhouse failed, the sufferer could always turn to Swayne's Tar and Sarsaparilla Pills, which were offered as a patent cure for "headache, constipated bowels, inward piles, costiveness, fevers, torpid liver, yellowness of skin and eyes, indigestion, dyspepsia, and all derangements of the internal viscera," a comprehensive catalog of the ills then prevalent. The advertisement for this panacea made clear that "unlike many other purgatives they [the pills] do not irritate the stomach and bowels," but keep "the system in . . . healthy condition by arousing (sic) the torpid liver to healthy action in expelling by the bowels and kidneys the matter that poisons the foundations of life." A thorough dose of Swayne's Pills must have been quite an experience.

Weakened by hard work, poor food, and patent medicines, the miners fell easy victims to the smallpox which broke out during the summer of 1876. By August new cases were reported every day. The women of Deadwood organized a committee to care for the destitute sick and ably solicited donations for this good cause. The city government built a smallpox hospital, or pest house, in which to quarantine the patients. Fortunately the disease was in a mild form, and the epidemic was over before its presence could discourage immigration to the Hills.

Having discussed the way in which men lived, let us now look at the way they earned their living. Not all were fortunate enough to find a paying mine; most had to work for others or go into business for themselves. Wages for skilled miners varied from $4.00 to $7.00 a day, and since only half a dozen men could work efficiently at the average placer operation, the owners generally preferred to pay high wages and get the best men available. Inexperienced miners, when they could get work at all, received from $1.00 to $3.00 a day and board. Jobs were scarce and probably not more than one-third of the men in Deadwood were permanently employed.

The unemployed pilgrim could find a number of things to do. Often his friends supported him in idleness, for an extra hand was always useful, if only to go along with each new stampede to stake out claims for his busier companions. Hunting, too, was a pleasant avocation which supplied food for one's friends, and often an income, for the successful usually sold their game to restaurants or to other miners. In a last extremity a man could always beg like "Swill Barrel Jimmy," who affected a shabby frock coat and a clean paper collar, but was supported by the generosity of Main Street restaurants which gave him leftovers and tablescraps. An enterprising man could go into business on his own, like the "Bottle Fiend" whose shack was surrounded by tubs and barrels of empty bottles which he offered for sale.

Whatever the transaction, gold dust was the medium of exchange. It could be converted to greenbacks only at a discount. Gold dust commanded a higher price than bills of exchange, for it was assumed to be worth $20 an ounce, when actually the price of even refined gold was considerably less. Local merchants of course compensated for the artificially high price of gold dust by charging correspondingly high prices for their goods. Lastly, making a purchase with "dust" was a good way to impress visitors with the wealth and gold production of the Hills.

Gold scales and a "blower," or shallow tin pan in which sand and trash could be blown out of the dust, were essential business equipment. The scale was only used for major transactions, because a practiced clerk or bartender could pick up an accurate fifty cents' worth of gold dust between his thumb and forefinger. Some of the dust generally spilled, so the thoughtful put a small square of carpeting under the scales and blower to catch it. After a good day's business this "side money" might amount to as much as a ten dollar addition to a bartender's salary.

The gold, once collected and taken to the bank, was shipped to New York where it sold for $17.50 per ounce, less 1½ percent for stage- and rail-transportation charges. In the summer of 1877 the Deadwood merchants agreed among themselves to reduce the price of gold dust from $20 to $18 an ounce, but the uproar made by the miners forced a return to the old rate. By the summer of 1879, however, a more business-like arrangement was accepted, with gold valued according to its source: Deadwood dust brought $17.10 per ounce, and the purer product from Rapid and Castle creeks brought $18.25.

The first bank in Deadwood, managed by J. M. Wood, dealt mainly in gold, exchanging it for greenbacks at a discount of 10 per cent, or storing it in a safe at a charge of 1 per cent a month. One tenderfoot arrived in camp with his money tied up in Wells Fargo certificates—the predecessors of modern traveler's checks—and changed them at the bank for gold dust for a 5 per cent charge. Leaving the Hills a week later and wanting his assets in more portable form, he had to buy back the same certificates at another discount.

Transactions like these quickly brought in competing bankers and correspondingly lowered charges. There was still profit enough for all, for banking business often exceeded $100,000 a day. The price paid for gold was based on the New York market, less a profit of $2 an ounce when the gold was "coined" and credited to the bank's account. As hard-rock mills increased in number, dust gradually gave way to gold bars about 1 by 2½ by 8 inches in size and worth approximately $3,000 each. Jovial bankers often told small children that they could have one if they could lift it off the table, but the sloping sides of the bars made this feat impossible.

When the town board of Deadwood took a business census in September, 1876, the list revealed twenty-seven saloons, twenty-one groceries, fourteen gambling houses, and eleven haberdasheries, out of a total of 166 establishments. Also, there were five peanut-roasters and one soda-water plant. Surprisingly, butter was big business. One retailer sold eighteen tons of it in three months. Eggs, too, were a promising speculation. The Gardner brothers brought in several thousand from Yankton during the winter of 1876. They were individually wrapped in paper and then packed in barrels of oats. The barrels were stacked in wagons, and the interstices between them filled with more oats to protect the cargo from breakage and freezing. The Gardners' wagon train consisted of thirty wagons, twelve of which carried lumber and the rest eggs, flour, pork, and butter. Cigars also came in by the wagonload, but the *Pioneer* deplored the growing sale of deleterious and effeminate cigarettes which were then just becoming popular.

Charles Sasse and Jacob Shoudy started a butcher shop early in the spring of 1876 when they bought a few crippled oxen that could not make the trip back to the states. They quickly built up a thriving meat and ranching business. Trade was brisk in horses, too. The villainous Charley "Red" Clark, who helped promote a stampede to the Wolf Mountains in 1876 in order to sell his excess stock, ran one stable. Wes Travis ran another. The latter advertised his merchandise by riding up and down the streets on a bucking, pitching bronco, ending up at his own corral, where he often sold his gentler animals to customers attracted by the performance.

"Corners" on various commodities were a common way to lose friends and make money. Jim Wardner, a notorious speculator, bought up all the grain in town during the summer of 1879 and hoped to make a killing during the winter. His warehouse, unfortunately, burned to the ground during the great Deadwood Fire. He recouped his losses by speculating in fresh eggs which he bought in Iowa for $4.50 a case and sold in Deadwood for $15. "Coal Oil Johnny" Spencer cornered the kerosene market and tripled the price to $3.75 a gallon. His customers complained, but paid. Perhaps it was this sort of commercial practice, as well as the prospect of mining litigation, that attracted over fifty lawyers to Deadwood. Even so, there was not enough business for all of them, and many had to find other jobs. One lawyer, for example, dealt faro at the Melodeon, and another worked the windlass on a nearby mining claim.

Once the gold rusher had established himself in his mine, job, or business, he began to look around for entertainment. Depending on how hard he searched, he could find almost anything he wanted, from the coarsest saloons and bawdy houses to libraries and literary societies.

The most popular institution of entertainment, sociability, and refreshment was the saloon. It was, of course, totally illegal, for until 1877 the Hills were part of an Indian reservation where liquor technically was outlawed. One malefactor, Fritz Drogmund, was actually convicted and punished for having sold it. His example, however, did not deter other bartenders, who were ever willing to risk fines in order to provide the miners with cooling and sustaining beverages. It was a great relief to all when in June, 1876, the U.S. commissioner in charge of enforcing the law decided that it was all right to bring liquor onto the reservation, just as long as none of it was sold to the Indians.

The first saloon in Deadwood was run by Ike Brown, who also owned the adjoining grocery store. Across both buildings he put a sign "Zion's Cooperative Mercantile Institution," indicating that he adhered, at least in part, to Mormon principles. Other saloons quickly followed, until by July, 1877, there were seventy-five in town. Their managers, if not already corrupt, rapidly became so, and practiced every skullduggery they could devise for the rapid separation of the miner and his money. The drunk who ordered "drinks for the house" without the dust to pay for them found himself in the street, unless he could persuade the bartender to accept a watch, overcoat, or other valuables instead of money. Instances of such transactions were fairly frequent; ill-disposed persons have even claimed that some of the bartenders accepted goods worth more than the bill and even encouraged their customers in their riotous extravagance.

Coexisting with the saloon was the gambling house. Most of the professional gamblers put on a good, raucous show, like the white-haired old fellow who urged "Come on up, boys, and put your money down—everybody beats the old man—the girls all beat the old man—the boys all beat the old man—everybody beats the old man—forty years a gambler—the old fool—everybody beats the old man—put your money down, boys, and beat the old man." He was not as big a fool as he pretended for he usually ended up with all the money.

Women, too, acted as dealers at many of the gaming tables, "and more resembled incarnate fiends than did their vulture-like male associates." Most of the miners preferred to play with men, for "the women were generally old and unscrupulous hands whose female subtlety made them paramount in all the devices of cheating and theft." Most of the gambling games were said to be honest, but from the popularity of faro, a game at which the dealer has practically no percentage if honestly played, it seems unlikely."

The man who did not spend his money on liquor or lose it gambling often managed to spend it on loose women. Dance halls, known as "hurdy-gurdy houses," soon sprang up to provide this opportunity. The first dance hall opened on May 1, 1876, with only the proprietor's wife and daughter to entertain its customers, but it soon added six more women of more questionable virtue. Within the month two more dance halls were available, and these were quickly joined by variety theaters wherein a customer might be entertained by the woman of his choice in the clandestine privacy of a curtained box.

The most notorious of the dance-hall proprietors was Al Swearingen, owner of the Gem Theater. He first established himself in Custer, but then moved with the miners to the riper fields of Deadwood Gulch. Swearingen made frequent trips to the East to recruit young women for his business, promising them respectable employment as "waiter girls" or actresses, only to force them into an abandoned life of shame when they reached Deadwood. An ordinary night's business at the Gem amounted to $5,000, and on occasion reached twice that figure, yet Swearingen died broke, killed in Denver while trying to hitch a ride on a freight train. The Gem, however, "continued to the end in maintaining its notorious record as a defiler of youth, a destroyer of homes, and a veritable abomination."

To keep order in places like the Gem, the *Deadwood Daily Times* proposed a monthly "fine or license fee" which would not only replenish the city treasury, but would have "a most salutary effect in driving women of the street out of town or into the house of a responsible madame." These establishments were generally in the news. In one, for example, a woman named "Tricksie" was beaten by her lover. She snatched up a pistol and shot him, the bullet passing through his head behind the eyes. Fortunately, there were no brains, at least in that section of his skull, and he recovered in a few weeks.

Another Deadwood girl had a specially embroidered dress, ornamented with the brands and initials of her admirers. Some of the initials caressed her shoulders and ample bosom, some occupied only outlying portions of this novel garment, while others were so placed as to be frequently sat upon. As her affection for each lover dictated where she placed his mark, a man could tell at a glance just what she thought of his attentions.

Many of these gay ladies were well known in town. Judge Granville Bennett gravely tipped his hat as he passed them, saying, from the eminence of his magisterial dignity, "I can afford to." Mrs. Bennett did her best to reform some of the less willing victims of a life of sin, and in this noble work she was assisted by a few kindhearted madames. Some successes were obtained, for as one madame said, "some girls just don't make good prostitutes." Other citizens pretended to ignore this seamy side of Deadwood's social life as beneath their notice.

The poor girls who remained in the business did not last long. Within two or three years drink, drugs, crime, and disease removed them from their supposedly glamorous life. Many deaths reported in the newspaper as pneumonia or fever were actually due to laudanum or a lover's bullet. Only a few of the facts, however, seeped through to plague the conscience of the town. The deaths of Emma Worth, from an overdose of morphine, or of Katie Smith, madame of the Hidden Treasure Number Two, from the same cause, made only a ripple on the surface of Deadwood's so-called high society.

The forces of morality gradually prevailed. "Colorado Charley" Utter was brought before the district court in 1879 on a charge of keeping a "nuisance" in Lead City. One witness, disposed to describe in detail the cancan dance which one of Utter's girls performed, was quickly silenced by the judge. It did not matter, said his honor, just how high the poor girl kicked—the main point was that Utter's house permitted gambling, drinking, boisterous talk, and men and women "herding together like animals." Without further qualification he declared it a nuisance which ought to be closed.

Years later the good people of South Dakota prohibited the sale of spirituous liquors in their state, and the once-thriving dens of immorality faded one by one. Young Carl Leedy, meeting the proprietress of one of Rapid City's leading houses, asked her if she planned to reopen her establishment. "Kid," she replied succinctly, "you can't run a sporting house on creek water!"

The theater, except when debased by the addition of bars, gambling, and wild women, as in the Gem and other "variety" houses, provided more cultivated entertainment. The leading actor in the Hills was Jack Langrishe, who came to Deadwood with his troupe in July, 1876. He quickly built a theater, roofed it with slats and canvas, and opened it for business. Seats consisted of stakes driven into the ground and topped with pieces of board. Admission to the first performance, Brownson Howard's *Banker's Daughter*, cost $1.50. A violent thunderstorm poured water through the makeshift roof and drenched players and audience alike, but did not stop the show. Whenever business was slack, Langrishe wrote for the *Pioneer* or panned gold from his own placer claim. He stayed in town through many vicissitudes until September 2, 1879. While in Deadwood he and his competitors presented a total of 168 plays, one-half of which were drama, the rest comedies and a few light operas.

Not even the melodrama of the 1870's could equal the dramatic impact of one performance at the Melodeon. "Handsome Banjo Dick" Brown and his partner, Fanny Garrettson, were in the midst of their act when a dim figure staggered to the footlights, muttered incoherently, and hurled an ax upon the stage. Brown coolly drew his pistol and shot the attacker dead. He was found to be Ed Shaunessey of Laramie, Miss Garrettson's discarded lover, who had come to Deadwood with the hope of regaining her affections. Miss Garrettson, or, as she then styled herself, Mrs. Brown, wrote to the papers to stifle a malicious rumor that she had once been Shaunessey's wife. This, she said, was totally untrue, for though she had lived with him for three years, they had never married, and so there was nothing immoral about her having run away with Mr. Brown.

Historians have frequently used a reputed 130-day run of the *Mikado* in Deadwood as evidence of culture on the mining frontier. Since the Gem could seat five hundred customers, such a phenomenal performance assumes that every person in the Hills attended between three and four times. Actually, the *Mikado* was not written until 1885, and the whole story is based on a brief description in Estelline Bennett's *Old Deadwood Days*. The Gem really did put on a series of Gilbert and Sullivan burlesques in 1887, but the costumes, or lack thereof, were apparently the main attraction.

Sundays were the miners' shopping days. As many as three thousand ragged, unwashed, and boisterous men and women crowded into Deadwood's narrow, muddy main street, eager for excitement. All stores remained open (the saloons never closed), and only a curbside preacher or two and a few onlookers served to remind passers-by of the true nature of the day.

Other than Sundays, the first great celebration in the Hills (was) the Fourth of July, 1876. The miners wanted to have a holiday for their own enjoyment, and in addition wished to show their numbers, patriotism, and prosperity in order that the federal government might extend recognition and protection from the hostile Indians. Beginning at midnight, July 3, the miners patriotically fired one hundred cannon salutes. A tall liberty pole gaily flaunted an assortment of rags made from garments of "mystical sublimity," donated by the ladies of the city. Judge W. L. Kuykendall presided over the oratorical effusions, which included the reading of the Declaration of Independence by General A. R. Z. Dawson, the federal revenue collector, and the presentation of a petition asking Congress for help and protection. Montana City and Elizabethtown, down the gulch, had their own celebrations. The day was concluded with a Grand Ball at the Grand Central Hotel.

The local newspaper was one of the most effective means of spreading culture and decorum on the mining frontier. Most of the early papers were founded in the hope that publication of mining-claim notices would provide a steady income, for federal law required such publication. The miners, however, blithely ignored this technicality and worked their mines with no legal assistance other than the approval of their neighbors. The papers had also hoped that the publication of notices for corporations, towns, and counties would keep them going, but this business, too, either failed to materialize or was dissipated among competitors without profiting anyone in particular.

A weekly edition of the *Cheyenne Daily Leader* was the first paper issued specifically for the Hills. It began printing news from the mines on May 1, 1876, under startling headlines such as: "Nuggets of News from the Ledges and Gulches," or "Golden Breezes Wafted Southward from the Treasure Vaults."

At least four efforts were made to start a paper in Custer. Around March 1, 1876, two "blacksmiths" (heavy-handed, incompetent printers) left Cheyenne to go into the business, but were evidently unsuccessful. A week later printers W. A. Laughlin and A. W. Merrick arrived in Custer, but decided to go on to Deadwood when Captain C. V. Gardner offered to finance the move. James Thorn brought a press from Nebraska City, Nebraska, only to abandon his editorial efforts at Cheyenne. The *Custer Herald,* edited by J. S. Bartholomew, began publication in October, but, as previously mentioned, eventually moved northward to Central City. Lastly, the *Custer Chronicle,* which continues to the present, was begun early in 1880.

In Deadwood, the *Black Hills Pioneer,* which was first issued on June 8, 1876, soon ran into difficulties. A shortage of newsprint forced it to print some issues on wrapping paper and various shades of handbill stock. A competitor, the *Black Hills Daily Times,* edited by W. P. Newhard and Porter Warner, appeared April 7, 1877. In 1897 it merged with the *Pioneer,* forming the paper which still serves the community. Charles Collins, the Sioux City editor who had done so much to publicize the Hills, came to Deadwood and on June 2, 1877, started the *Black Hills Champion.* In the fall the *Deadwood Miner* appeared briefly, followed in the spring of 1878 by Captain Gardner's *Mining and Real Estate Journal.*

Neighboring towns, too, had their journals. The *Black Hills Tribune,* published in Crook City by X. S. Burke, appeared once, June 9, 1876, but was never heard from again. In Carbonate Camp, a new silver town northwest of Deadwood, the *Carbonate Reporter* had boomed and collapsed by the end of 1881. Bartholomew's *Central City Herald* was joined by the *Register* in 1878, and in 1879 by the Reverend B. Fay Mills' *Central Christian,* which the *Deadwood Times* described as "editorially well gotten up, but typographically . . . awful." In Lead the *Sunday Register, Lead City Telegraph,* and *Western Enterprise* competed with each other for the meager news of that rather sober city.

Outlying communities also had their papers. In Rapid City, Joseph Gossage began the *Black Hills Journal,* which today serves the whole of South Dakota west of the Missouri. Mr. W. D. Knight published at least two editions of the *Rockerville Black Hills Miner,* apparently using a press bought from the defunct *Crook City Tribune.* At Rochford the *Black Hills Central,* and later the *Rochford Miner,* consisted mainly of "boiler plate" (preset advertisements) and "patent insides" (preprinted paper with one side left to be filled with local news and editorials). To these were added the poetry of H. N. Maguire and T. F. Walsh, as well as excerpts from the former's books on the Black Hills.

The most civilizing influence of all was the church. Preacher Henry Weston Smith delivered his first sermon in the Hills at Custer on May 7, 1876, and then moved on to Deadwood with the rush. He usually spoke out of doors, standing on a packing box with his hat at his feet to receive contributions. One day "Calamity Jane" Cannary took the hat and passed it through the crowd bellowing, "You sinners, dig down in your pokes now; this old fellow looks as though he were broke and I want to collect about two hundred dollars for him." She did, too. When Smith was killed on his way to preach at Crook City, Jane summed up the public reaction pretty well: "Ain't it too bad the Indians killed the only man that came into the Hills to tell us how to live. And we sure need the telling."

The Congregational Church, represented by the Reverend L. P. Norcross, came early to Deadwood and held services wherever it could—in a butcher shop, in the dining room of the Centennial Hotel, or in a carpenter shop. It ultimately built a church in January 1877.

Father Lonergan, the Catholic priest, also used a carpenter shop when he celebrated the first Mass in May, 1877. The Episcopalians borrowed Jack Langrishe's theater for their services.

One Sunday, Billy Nuthall, proprietor of the Melodeon, allowed the Reverend W. L. Rumney to hold services in his bar. Gambling equipment was pushed to one side, while Rumney, an ex-Confederate officer, preached from the vaudeville stage. When the sermon was over, "Nutshell Bill," a well-known gambler, spoke up saying, "Now boys, the old man has been telling you how to save your souls; come this way and I'll show you how to win some money."

Unfortunately, Deadwood was not populated solely by men who thirsted for religion. Some even did their best to still further enliven the already boisterous entertainment available in the local bars and gambling houses. Others, impoverished and corrupted by drink and dissipation, turned to a life of crime and became the badmen, murderers, and road agents who did so much to make life in the Hills a varied and exciting experience.

"Deadwood in the Spring of 1877"
Chicago Times / Adams Museum
May 1877

The following account, first published in the Chicago Times *in May 1877, comes from a cub reporter who stopped in Deadwood in the first spring of its youth, when the town's predominant feature was mud. Virtually overnight, gold camps were established and thousands flocked to the prospect of a better tomorrow. In a matter of weeks, the Deadwood-Whitewood area boasted a population of 5,500. In this brief dispatch, the* Chicago Times' *reporter captures his perceptions of a town just born—a place of guns and grit and gold.*

I have had leisure to-day to view the town, or as much thereof as the mud will permit. And writing of mud, you people that are back in the states that are prone to growl at your commissioners and officials generally, should you chance to discover a layer or two of filth upon the streets, you would be speechless could you stand upon any of Deadwood's boulevards and see the spectacle presented at this time. Mud? The main street is bottomless, and is navigated by our "prairie schooners" only by the exercise of the utmost navigational skill. Horses are coated with mud; vehicles pass along; nothing visible but a flapping ear or two belonging to buried mules and the "poop-deck" of the craft to which they are attached. Six and eight mules and horses are before every wagon, and find difficulty in moving it even when empty. The Sidney stage came in to-day drawn by six horses so completely covered with mud that their color could not be determined. The passengers were swimming along on foot. Pedestrianism is attended with great danger, for the few miserable structures called sidewalks are inches deep in slippery mud, and every step throws up a shower as from some huge atomizer. Three great mill-ponds apparently ornament the street, drainage being stopped by crosswalks.

In its infancy, Deadwood's Main Street was a scene of ramshackle huts, temporary tents, ox carts, and mud so deep it could claim a man. Over the next century, the region was awash in glittering gold, and modern amenities and Sunday socials soon followed. (Photo courtesy of the Adams Museum, Deadwood, SD)

Amid all this floundering, slipping, and splashing and showering of mud, what could be more ridiculously absurd than to see a valiant boot-black approach a great burly "bull-whacker," the former's variegated garments mud from collar to boot-tops, while the latter's are dripping with slime, and innocently accost him with a "Shine sir; shine 'em up?"

Notwithstanding the heavy condition of all roads leading into the hills, arrivals from all parts of the country are very numerous, and are becoming more so each day. Stages come in loaded down, and report hundreds of pilgrims en route on foot and in private vehicles. Every hotel and boarding house is constantly crowded to the utmost, and nightly turns away scores of applicants for accommodations. Building is going on as I never saw before, and the sound of the saw and the hammer is heard by night and by day. Every thing here is purely marvelous, and so different from the accustomed sights of more ancient parts that the new arrival stands and gazes in utter astonishment. A single game of poker drew into sight $1,200 in dust last evening, and continued until nine this morning. In the same room several faro games and other devices for gambling purposes were surrounded with apparently happy crowds. They bet, win, and lose with the utmost nonchalance, and whatever way fortune smiles they conclude with a smile over the bar, a smile for every acquaintance, and smilingly depart. There is no rowdyism, no disorder—peace and happiness prevails.

A BROTHER'S LETTER
JANUARY 1878

*Presented as written, run-on sentences and misspellings fully in atten-
dance, the following letter from George Robinson to his brother, Stewart,
in the long winter of 1878, tells a tale of hard work and struggle. But in
his missive, George also finds time to smile at himself and his friends,
who spend the deep freeze gambling and drinking in the local saloons.*

*In his own earthy way, George warns his brother not to make the
treacherous trek to Dakota Territory without ample evidence of paying claims, "for there (are) thousands of Poor Men out here." He then
explains that many of his fellow placer miners spent their stake just
getting to the Hills, found no gold, and now are relegated to working
solely for their room and board, stuck in a vicious cycle.*

*In his earnest way, at letter's end, George makes clear his longing
for home, family, and friends, rather than the back-breaking work of
gold mining he has come to know so intimately in the Black Hills of
Dakota Territory.*

January 10th, 1878

Dead Wood D.T.

Dear Brother

I received your kind & welcom Letter & was much pleased to find
you well as this is the first of the year. I will give you a little histry of
Deadwood Im now writing in Meortons Club Room & there is a bout
200 Men here & purty much all Gambling. Some Playing Faroh &
some Rolet & some Poker & them that is not Gambling is a bout how
Come you So, Jes Barton he got Drunk & fell off the steps & skined
his Face he is a nice speciman.

& the People is some what excited there is a big Band of Indins
in the Belfoos break a bout 40 Meiles from here think they will take
Spare Fish.

Placer miners toil in the creek of Deadwood Gulch. Some prospectors became rich, while others moved on to better claims. (Photo courtesy of the Adams Museum, Deadwood, SD)

This week the Father D. E. Smit Meine sold for $400,000 & the Wolsey Meine holds theres at $1000000, so you Can se that there is some very extensive Meines in the Black Hills I think I have some just as good but Stewart it takes time for to Develope Quarts Meines a specily a poor boys like me I have sunk 5 Shafts a bout 25 ft. deepe & they Essay from 6 to $20 per Ton which is Rich for surface Rock

I can not do eney thing more at them till Spring for the Snow is deap & Cold sometimes quartz Pinch Out Mine May but Im giving

mine a thurvny test if they proove good I will give you a good Show
but Stewart do not come to the Hills unless they should be good for
ther thousand of Poor Meen out here came to the Hills & did expect
to ppick up a Fraction with out work & can Not get bqack home &
Run wages down & works for ther Bord.

You sed Frank had rented the Farm is going to take on the Lora
Hick I herd he was paying his Dilresses to her & hoo is Lon Charnny
& how is my Sallie I have not wrote to her sins I Left Omaha hope
She is Right End up with Care.

This is all at present Please write soon

Love to all from your Brother George

"Doomed: The Rise & Fall of Deadwood's Chinatown"
Deadwood Magazine
Dustin D. Floyd
February 2006

Unlike the Chinese populations prevalent in San Francisco and other nineteenth-century U.S. metropolises, Deadwood's Chinatown has received scant attention, save the occasional master's thesis. But, the Chinese played a major role in the founding, development, and evolution of the booming gold camp, drawn to the opportunity to strive and struggle, to stutter, and then, seemingly against all odds, to succeed in this promised land on the western frontier.

Often unwilling to risk potential confrontation with well-armed white miners, Chinese immigrants to the Black Hills, who once numbered in the hundreds, excelled in operating restaurants, boardinghouses, and the ever-present laundries. Still others ran groceries, bakeries, stables, gambling halls, and opium dens. Few remnants remain of Deadwood's Chinatown in the form of buildings, but twenty-first-century archaeological digs have yielded a treasure trove of several thousand artifacts ranging from firearms and bottles to gaming pieces and military medals.

Oxford-educated Dustin D. Floyd, executive editor of Deadwood Magazine, *tells the tale of the Chinese in Deadwood in this February 2006 feature, written in the wake of the unauthorized destruction of the town's Wing Tsue buildings. In his account, Floyd shines his literary light on Chinese life in a burgeoning gold camp, the rise of respected merchant Fee Lee Wong, and U.S. immigration laws that led to the inevitable decline of the Chinese population of Deadwood.*

More than half of the lots sit vacant along a lonely two-block stretch of Black Hills road. A layer of crushed rock covers most of the empty land, making life difficult for the few dandelion tenants that take root in the spring. A century ago this was a thriving community with its own court of justice, religious buildings, police force and fire department. Now the once-bustling burg is all but abandoned, with only three buildings left standing—none of which date from its turn-of-the-century heyday.

But this ghost town isn't located at the bottom of some forsaken valley, nor is it lost at the top of a mountain peak where the gold mines ran dry long ago. Once known as Chinatown, this forgotten city sits in the very center of Deadwood, where upwards of two million visitors unknowingly stroll through it each year.

At its peak, the boundaries of Deadwood's Chinatown stretched from the present intersection of Main Street and U.S. 85 to the location of the modern Mineral Palace Hotel. Grocers, boarding houses, bakeries, opium dens, gambling halls and stables lined the street in between, which bustled with the noise of several hundred residents. The ubiquitous Chinese laundry was there too, and several more were conveniently scattered throughout the city. Leading businessmen organized rival hose teams, a type of volunteer fire department that also doubled as an athletic team in celebratory foot races. A joss house served as both a temple and a court of law. Emporiums sold foods, spices and medicines imported from China—true luxuries, given the 7,300-mile journey by ship, rail and wagon. The more Deadwood prospered, the more Chinatown grew.

But Deadwood's prosperity couldn't compete with national sentiment. A flurry of anti-immigration laws kept the town's largely bachelor Chinese population from replenishing itself. At the same time, the ethnic enclaves or larger urban centers on America's coasts grew in size, enticing the Chinese living in the Black Hills with the promise of new economic opportunities. Deadwood's Chinatown shrunk significantly following the birth of the 20th century, and by 1940 there were only two known persons of Chinese origin in the entirety of Lawrence County.

Though visibly faded, the community has never been entirely erased from Deadwood. Fueled by a mix of history and local legend, the rise and fall of Chinatown still exudes an influence over the city today, beckoning to residents and visitors alike with its historically exotic allure.

Gold Mountain

While the Chinese immigrants who flooded into the United States during the latter half of the 19th century came from a culture utterly foreign to the American Frontier, they had the same reasons for migrating as most white pioneers: gold. The bloody Taiping Rebellion, which claimed upwards of 20 million lives between 1851 and 1864, sandwiched by the Opium Wars with Britain, created miserable living conditions for many in China. News of California's 1849 gold rush infused hope into the hearts of the common people, who began referring to America as *gam saan* (金山), or gold mountain.

Filled with visions of wealth and an easier life, tens of thousands began making the perilous four-month journey across the ocean on clipper ships and older sailing vessels. The $200 to $300 price of passage was steeper than many Chinese could afford, and occasionally up to 20% of the passengers would die en route. The dangers did little to discourage waves of Chinese immigrants, who engaged in prospecting, laboring and general commerce.

But as the placer deposits petered out on America's West Coast, prospectors moved inland toward other gold discoveries. The 1876 rush to the Black Hills, the last of the nation's major gold rushes, attracted thousands of eager miners, including many of Chinese origin. Coupled with a national financial crisis caused by the Panic of 1873, the rich placer claims of Deadwood seem to offer the perfect financial opportunity.

"You have a recession going on, and the announcement that gold has been discovered, and the Chinese, like everyone else, were very eager to capitalize on that announcement," explains Mary Kopco, director of the Adams Museum and House in Deadwood. "Many came to set up businesses to service the mining camp, and others came to work the placers."

However, census figures indicate that only a small portion of Deadwood's Chinese were engaged in mining. Most chose to operate restaurants, boarding houses, the ubiquitous laundry and other service-related businesses, perhaps in an effort to avoid the unpleasant confrontations with jealous white prospectors that marked many other Western gold camps.

"They did the placer mining as much as the local miners would allow them," says Eileen French, an amateur local historian. "There was resistance, just like we have resistance to immigration today. People feel threatened."

"Where you see the hatred and animosity is where the Chinese come and work the mines," echoes David Wolff, an associate professor of history at Black Hills State University. "Now some of the Chinese did work claims on lower Whitewood Creek. But the sense is that everyone thought, 'Well, they're so far down there, that's the worst mining ground anyway.' And it was pretty bad for mining, but some of them did pretty well."

The success of Chinese miners was significant enough to make the newspapers of the day, which reported on October 4, 1878, that one fortunate immigrant had discovered "a nugget on his claim that weighed over four hundred dollars." A few months later the *Black Hills Daily Times* wrote that a certain group of Chinese using sluices "have been taking out at the rate of $4 to the heathen, while the white miners were unable to make the water run."

Liping Zhu, associate professor of history at Eastern Washington University, points to several reasons for the achievements of Chinese prospectors. "A spirit of teamwork, water management skills, nutritious diets, advanced healthcare and environmental adaptation abilities all contributed to the success," he wrote in *Ethnic Oasis: The Chinese in the Black Hills.*

Laundries were one of the more popular business choices for the Chinese in Deadwood, due to their low start-up costs (less than $20, according to Zhu), low overhead (water from the creek and wood from the forest were free) and high profit potential. Zhu notes that most miners were taking in between $4 and $7 per day in the late 1870s, while a savvy laundry operator could make $10 or better.

In fact, the Chinese held a virtual monopoly on laundry business in Deadwood for several decades—a business advantage they protected with a vengeance. After years of complaining about the high prices of laundry services, Deadwood residents rejoiced in 1880 when two white women built their own laundry establishment in town. The Chinese laundries responded by severely underselling their new competition, who soon went out of business—at which point the Chinese brought their rates back up to previous levels.

Finding a Niche

Of course, limiting their engagement in mining didn't completely shield Deadwood's Chinese community from discrimination and injustice. Black Hills historian Watson Parker notes several examples of this attitude in *Deadwood: The Golden Years*. In one case, an article in the 1876 *Cheyenne Leader* described a fictional group made up of "Hop-Lee, Ding-Dong, Heap-Wash and Hang-Jeff, Celestial chuckle-heads from the Flowery kingdom" who were headed to the gold fields of Deadwood. Parker also describes a time when local attorney Henry Frawley once defended a white man for murdering a Chinese resident. The crux of his defense was that no law prohibited the slaying of a Chinese person, and suggested the lesser charge of "cruelty to animals," which carried a $25 fine. The judge agreed.

The *Black Hills Daily Times* of March 26, 1881, reveals further discrimination in the form of a quarterly tax exclusively on Deadwood's laundries in the amount of $10. Zhu notes that the Chinese were outraged at the idea, and when the justice of the peace went out to collect the fees he found that the laundry owners had relocated their business signage to various vacant buildings.

But Deadwood's attitude toward its Chinese community appeared to change over the years. Discrimination and antagonism seemed to lessen, and the cases of tension seen in court documents and newspaper articles grew fewer in number. Zhu credits Granville Bennett, a highly respected lawyer and judge, and Sol Star, a businessman and 22-year mayor of Deadwood, with helping to integrate the city's Chinese and white residents.

"Over the years you see a little more interaction between the Chinese and white communities," Wolff explains. "That indicates a sense of harmony."

Nowhere is this interaction more apparent than in the case of Fee Lee Wong, an early Chinese immigrant who turned his Wing Tsue emporium and mining interests into a small fortunate. Deadwood's white residents often frequented his store, and soon embraced his family into the broader community.

"That's one of the things that's so fascinating about Deadwood," says French. "Fee Lee Wong was very much accepted into the white community. He became a Black Hills Pioneer in the 1890s. A Chinaman in a white organization? That's unheard of."

The depth of Deadwood's attachment to Wong was made plain in 1904. Following a two-year trip to China, Wong was detained by bureaucratic immigration officials on his return voyage and temporarily denied permission to enter the United States. When the news reached Deadwood, citizens were outraged.

"The people in town, when Fee Lee was arrested, they went to their congressman and said, 'Let our Chinaman go!'" French says. "I don't know that he would have liked being treated a bit like being property, but they were all very proud of him."

Chinatown's Demise

But Deadwood's gradual acceptance of its Chinatown wouldn't be enough to save it from its inevitable decline. Wong's short-lived

Fee Lee Wong & Family: Fee Lee Wong became one of Deadwood's most successful merchants and one of the few Chinese citizens who brought his family to the community. Pictured left to right are King Que, King Shiu, Hal Shek, infant Fay Juck, maid Shu Lin Lau, Fay King, Fee Lee, Som Quong, and Hong Quong. Tong Quong and Fay Lan were not yet born when this 1894 portrait was taken. (Photo courtesy of the Adams Museum, Deadwood, SD)

detention was the result of the 1882 Chinese Exclusion Act, a federal law designed to suppress immigration from China. With few people coming in to replenish the community—and only a small number of women to bear children—the existence of Deadwood's Chinatown came down to a game of numbers.

"Slowly you start to see the community erode and move to other places," Kopco says. "You also have the placer mines pinching out, and there are more opportunities and probably more stability in those urban areas."

"They responded to the market," Wolff adds. "We might make moves today based on how much we like a place, but it was different then. Historically speaking, your grandparents moved somewhere because there were better economic opportunities there. It was the same for the Chinese. It's a market force issue, I have to argue."

Some of Deadwood's Chinese moved to larger Chinatowns on the country's coasts, while others went back to their homeland. Wong fell into this latter category, making arrangements for a permanent return in 1918. He left the following year. Ching Ong, more commonly known as Teeter, is generally accepted as the last Chinese resident to leave Deadwood, having made his departure in 1931.

Few of the buildings in Deadwood's Chinatown were built to last. One by one, the abandoned structures were razed—some in the interest of public safety, others to make way for auto showrooms and other new businesses. By the late 1990s, the only visible remnants of Deadwood's Chinatown existed in the form of buildings constructed by the quarter's most powerful merchants. Wong's Wing Tsue store was the most obvious vestige of Chinatown until its apparently illegal destruction in December (2005).

However, the demolished Wing Tsue buildings may not have been the final architectural link to the city's Chinatown. Although denied by retiring Deadwood Historic Preservation Officer Jim Wilson, other historians and city officials confirm the remains of a store operated by Wong's biggest rival still stand next door. Known as the Hi Kee building, the structure apparently still stands at 560 Main Street.

"All the maps we have say it is the Hi Kee building," French asserts.

However, the building is currently occupied by the Main Street Deadwood Gulch casino, a business owned by the same individuals who allegedly razed the Wing Tsue buildings without authorization. Still, local historians are hopeful that whatever may remain of Deadwood's Chinatown will be recognized for its intrinsic value.

"That's our tangible connection to the history of this town," Wolff says. "People by the millions come to be a part of that history. They don't come here to read historic newspapers in an air-conditioned library . . . They come for the ambience of Deadwood. That's what our historic buildings provide—a tangible connection to what was."

"THE MURDER OF PREACHER SMITH"
FROM *PIONEER DAYS*
IN THE BLACK HILLS
JOHN S. MCCLINTOCK
1939

In the midst of the mud and the blood and the rot-gut whiskey that defined Deadwood in the spring of 1876, came an unusual man who sought to spread the word of God among those who desperately needed it. Though his time upon the stage of action was but brief, Henry Weston Smith—the "Pioneer Preacher"—left an indelible mark on the young town.

Today, Preacher Smith's contribution to the community is remembered by a memorial near the site of his murder, as well as his gravesite in Deadwood's Mount Moriah Cemetery.

One of the original pioneers in the Black Hills, John S. McClintock arrived in Deadwood just a month before Preacher Smith, searching for gold with the throng of itinerant miners who sought their personal fortunes. McClintock bore witness to the town's earliest days, settled there, and late in life, penned his memoirs.

At times as course as rough-hewn timber, McClintock dedicated his life's story to his "fellow plainsman and pioneers of the sixties and seventies, living or dead, who dared leave their homes and enter upon a crusade in defiance of the protests of hostile savages and the mandates of the Federal Government, to brave the dangers, endure the privations and sufferings even unto death, in their determination to enter into and to open to civilization vast areas of rich and unexplored regions of the Great Northwest."

But his book, Pioneer Days in the Black Hills, *provides an entertaining account of the gold rush, frequent confrontations with Indians, the legends of outlaws and road agents, and the real-life exploits of real Western characters, including Wild Bill Hickok, Calamity Jane,*

Deadwood Dick, Buckskin Johnny, Big Thumb Jake, and Madame Moustache, among others.

In the following excerpt, McClintock describes the mysterious death of one of Deadwood's favored sons, Preacher Smith, and the aftermath of his murder.

Of the many tragic incidents that marked the wildest days of '76 in this community, the one in particular by which the people were deeply and visibly affected, and which elicited many expressions of sorrow and regret, was that of the untimely death, by murder, of the Reverend Henry Weston Smith, the pioneer preacher of the Black Hills.

This pioneer preacher of the Gospel came to Ouster, in the southern part of the Black Hills, early in the spring of 1876, and worked at mining and other jobs before coming to Deadwood. Capt. C. V. Gardner relates that Smith joined one of his freight trains at Custer and came to Deadwood in May, 1876. Here he found employment with many others in the construction of the Boulder Ditch, a

In his short life Henry Weston Smith, the "Pioneer Preacher" of the Black Hills, left an indelible mark on Deadwood. (Photo courtesy of the Adams Museum, Deadwood, SD)

huge mushroom enterprise, that was vigorously pushed through to the finish of almost everybody and everything connected with the concern, except the ditch itself, which is yet unfinished and stands today as a monument to folly. It is not known whether or not Preacher

Smith received any compensation for his labor. It is known, however, that many others on the job did not.

My first contact with the Reverend Smith was on a Sunday shortly before his death. As I walked down Main Street I noticed a large gathering of men on the square at the end of Gold Street and heard someone speaking in a loud voice. Thinking only of auctioneers and street fakirs, I walked close to the speaker before I realized that I was in the presence of a minister of the Gospel, who was speaking in an easy, unaffected manner as though he might be at home addressing the members of his congregation. A score or two had hats off, listening intently to his discourse, while the great mass moved about restlessly, apparently paying but little attention to the speaker's remarks. However, no words were spoken to interrupt or embarrass him. Although I did not get his text, if he had given out any, I listened for a while to his sermon and was very favorably impressed by his manner and speech and unmistakable sincerity. I thought but little about the occurrence until after his murder, when I learned something of this man who had been toiling six days a week and traveling twenty miles on foot and preaching two sermons on the Sabbath. It was then that I realized, as I believe many others did, that the people of Deadwood had lost a man such as no community could afford to lose. I have since pictured the man who spoke to the multitude of people in the valley here, as a true disciple and an earnest follower in the footsteps of the Master who preached on the Mount nearly two thousand years before.

On Sunday, the 20th day of August, 1876, he delivered a sermon in the forenoon on Main Street, to the people of Deadwood; after which he started on foot and alone on his way to the town of Crook City for the purpose of preaching a sermon to the people later on the same day, as had been his custom for several Sundays. While on his way, traveling through timber at a point near the edge of Centennial Valley, and about five miles out from Deadwood, he was shot and killed. His body was discovered lying on the trail shortly afterwards by a man on horseback, who passed the body on his way to Crook City, where he made a report of the discovery.

A small party of men composed of Edmond Wolfe and others, immediately went to the place where the body lay. At that time Joseph Armstrong drove by with a hay wagon partly loaded with green hay. The body of the unfortunate preacher was placed on the hay and brought to Deadwood by Armstrong and given into the care of some friends and acquaintances, one of whom was C. E. Hawley, a highly respected churchman. He took charge of the remains, had them prepared for burial, and also conducted the funeral services at the grave, when all that was mortal of the good man was laid to rest in the new cemetery, which is now a residence portion of the Fourth Ward of Deadwood. His body, with nearly all others buried there, was removed some years later to a cemetery higher up on the mountain side, now known as Mount Moriah.

On the same day that the Reverend Smith was murdered, I was standing, in the afternoon, on Main Street between Gold and Wall streets in a group of men who were witnessing some amusing performances, when two horsemen came up the street on a gallop. I noticed something flapping against the shoulders of one of the horses and when they stopped within a few feet of where I stood, I saw that it was the head of an Indian tied to the horn of the saddle, either by the long hair or by a strap. It was not being dragged at the end of a rope as has been asserted by some and believed by many.

While the man who brought it was untying the head that bloodied the shoulder of the horse, he was asked the question, "Where did you get that thing?" He answered, "I killed him down the road." The next question was, "What are you going to do with it?" The answer came in a loud voice from someone on the outside, "Sell it at auction." This plan was agreed upon and one man mounted a platform that stood against the building and cried the sale. The first bid was low, but kept increasing until it reached twenty-five dollars and was knocked down at that bid. The "lucky man" who secured the gruesome prize was Dan Dority, general manager of that famous and unsavory institution known as the "Gem Theatre." If there was any money paid over I failed to see it, and I am certain that I witnessed the whole transaction. The parties to it went away down the street. I never afterwards saw the man who brought in the head. The statement was made by someone that he was a Mexican; this is generally believed, but I don't share in that belief. I stood close to the man and heard his words, which were few, and I detected no Mexican accent, nor did I think of a Mexican at that time. He was rather low in stature, having black hair, eyes, and beard. Apparently his age was about thirty. I afterwards learned that he was known as "Tex."

The head of the Indian sold at auction was kept for a time in a saloon until it ceased to be an object of curiosity or a wholesome ornament. It then was buried under the floor where it remained for about three years when it was exhumed while repairs to the building were being made. It was given to Louis Schoenfeld, who had had experience as an undertaker, and who roomed in my cabin. Louis dressed and polished the skull and hung it on the rail, where it kept vigil over us for many moons before he sent it by express to his former employer at Louisville, Kentucky. I could have kept it had I wished to do so.

On that same day a man by the name of Charles Mason was killed by an Indian at a point in the Whitewood Valley below Crook City. It was reported at the time, and the report afterwards was confirmed, that Mason had killed an Indian that same day before he himself was killed. The head of that Indian was brought into Deadwood that day by the impostor who claimed for himself the honor of killing the Indian.

A report of the confused affairs of that fatal day, which gained currency in later years, was that the body of Mason was brought to Deadwood and buried at the same time and in the same grave with that of Preacher Smith; and that afterwards both were removed and interred in the same grave on Mount Moriah. I was not present at the first burial, and am unable to vouch for the story. Although it was accepted as true by others, I gave the story little credence. However, I have never heard any other account of the burial of Mason.

Who killed the Rev. Henry Weston Smith? Practically all writers have charged the crime to Indians, and that has been the general belief.

No one saw the act committed. While first reports naturally attributed the killing to the Indians, no definite evidence was ever developed to support such belief. It is yet, and always will be, a matter of conjecture.

While this writer does not seek to controvert or change the fixed belief of those who accept the Indian theory, I long ago formed the opinion that it was done by a white man, for some unknown motive. In support of such belief may be cited that there is nothing in evidence that Indians were in that immediate vicinity that day, and the fact that the body was not scalped as was the invariable practice of the Indians of that day.

In 1891, a life-size statue was placed over Preacher Smith's grave in Mt. Moriah Cemetery. It was sculptured from red sandstone by J. B. Riordan, a New York sculptor who was in Deadwood temporarily at that time. It was sponsored by the local Methodist Church and was paid for by popular subscription. The sandstone being soft, the statue was badly chipped by relic hunters and defaced by weather, ere being enclosed.

In 1914 a monument was erected in honor of this pioneer preacher of the Gospel, on the Deadwood-Spearfish highway, about three miles from Deadwood. This is about two miles from the spot where he was killed, as was located by Edmond Wolfe, one of the men who picked up the body. Wolfe came to Deadwood from Wisconsin for that purpose in 1926, his expenses being paid by subscriptions from a number of citizens. He was accompanied on this locating trip by Mayor W. E. Adams, Editor E. L. Senn, Editor Earl Morford, this writer, and others.

The Smith Monument has become a shrine for Methodism. Every year since 1924 memorial services have been held there on a Sunday closely preceding or following the "Days of '76" celebration.

When the murdered martyr's body was searched after being brought to Deadwood, there was found in his pocket, scribbled on scraps of paper, outlines of the sermon he intended to preach at Crook City. They were sent, with other belongings, to his mother in Ohio. From these notes, the sermon was constructed as it would naturally have been delivered from the outline. A copy of this was obtained by Mrs. Frank Ickes of Deadwood from relatives, and was first read to the public on Main Street, Deadwood, during the "Days of '76" celebration in 1924 by Rev. W. E. Prewitt, pastor of the Deadwood Baptist Church, who impersonated the Reverend Smith. The undelivered sermon reads as follows:

Text: Romans 1:5.

The Apostle, next to Christ, may be considered as the most proper pattern for imitation by Christians of the present day.

Of all the disciples of the Lord, none seem to unite more of the graces of the Spirit of Paul.

Peter was zealous and impetuous, a son of thunder.

James was called "The Just."

John was full of gentleness and love.

Apollos was an eloquent speaker and Barnabas was a son of consolation.

But it was Paul alone who was able to become all things to all men. Among the excellencies of his character, none appear acre prominent than his self-sacrificing spirit and his devotion to the Gospel of Christ.

At the time of writing the language of the text he had already suffered severely in defense of the doctrines of Jesus of Nazareth; but still, while contemplating his journey to the very center of idolatry, to a city of luxury and pride, for the purpose of preaching the gospel of purity, temperance, and humility, and although he knew that he should, in all probability, be called to pass through as great trials as he already had perhaps to suffer death, he was still willing to serve God in any way at any time or place, and under any circumstances whatsoever, and declared "so as much as in me lies, I am ready to preach the gospel to you that are at Rome."

Now while we endeavor to gain instruction from the example of Paul, let us consider:

1. Why he was willing to do this.

2. Some of the ways in which we all may engage in this great work.

Why Was He Willing To Do This?

Answer, he loved God.

Before he embraced the religion of Jesus Christ, he was zealous toward God, and zealous of the honor of his religion. He believed that Christ was overthrowing the work of God, and he persecuted this way unto death. But when his mind was illuminated by the Holy Ghost, he saw that the honor of the gospel was the cause of God; he saw that this was the way in which God had determined to display the glories of His character. Paul saw in Christ the brightness of the Father's glory and the express image of His person. Him, of whom Moses and the prophets did write: "the chief among ten thousand, and altogether lovely." He saw displayed, in characters of fire, the holiness of God's law which had declared, "The soul that sinneth it shall die." Also His glorious justice, which sternly demanded the blood of the sinner and declared, "Without shedding of blood there is no remission."

He saw the glory of His wisdom in devising a plan by which He might be just and justify the sinner that believeth. He beheld the wonders of redeeming grace and undying love which led the Father to give His only begotten Son as a propitiation for our sins. He saw, indeed, the Divinity of Jesus Christ, in that depth of love which caused Him to leave the glory which He had with the Father, before the world was, and to take upon Himself of the seed of Abraham, to humble Himself and become obedient to death.

Being thus convinced that the glory of God and Christ was one, Paul gave himself to the work of spreading the news of Salvation in spite of bonds and afflictions, declaring "None of these things move me, neither count I my life dear unto myself, so that I might finish my course with joy and the ministry that I have received of the Lord Jesus, to testify the gospel of the grace of God."

Paul Loved His Fellow Men. He saw himself with all mankind ruined by sin and depravity, totally unable to regain the favor of God without the intervention of an Almighty Savior.

Here, in the gospel of the grace of God, was found the needed Savior—one able to save to the uttermost.

This was the reason he was not ashamed of the Gospel of Christ. He saw men in a state of spiritual death; if in Christ, life.

While the wrath was out against the sinner, He was made to sin for us who knew no sin. Mercy was free. Did the sinner find himself far from God by wicked works, he might be brought nigh by the blood of Christ; were he in darkness, Christ was light; were he sick of sin, Christ was a physician; would he return to God, Christ was the way; did he need gracious influences to lift him from the horrible pit of miry clay, Christ had promised that whatsoever he should ask in His name it should be given. "If ye then being evil, etc."

Although Paul verily once thought that he ought to do many things contrary to the will of Jesus of Nazareth, and while he was hating men and women and persecuting them, he verily thought he was doing God service; yet when he found that there was no other name given under heaven whereby we might be saved, and that through Him men might have everlasting life, Paul could say to all, 'Would to God that not only thou, but all that hear me this day were such as I am except these bonds.' And sometimes he did so long for the salvation of men that he could most wish himself accursed of Christ, cut off from all the blessings of the Gospel, if that would secure their salvation.

That men might take the blessings of the Gospel, He endured hunger and thirst, and cold and nakedness, stripes and buffetings.

Some Of The Ways In Which We May All Engage In The Great Work Of Preaching.

When our Savior said, "Go ye into all the world," He evidently intended the use of all means by which men may be

New York artist J.H. Riordan poses with his tribute to the "Pioneer Preacher of the Black Hills," Henry Westin Smith. Riordan created the statue in 1891 for Deadwood's Mount Moriah Cemetery. Tourists chipped away at the monument, hauling it away piece by piece until it eventually fell over in 1933. (Photo courtesy of Adams Museum, Deadwood, SD)

brought to a knowledge of the truth. All men are not called to stand up and preach as professed ministers of the Word. There are many ways for a Christian to follow Paul as he followed Christ; many ways in which we may assist in spreading abroad the story of the Cross.

First. Without money: Christ, sent His disciples forth without purse or scrip, but He did not intend that they should live without food.

Second. By sustaining the social needs of Grace.

All can do something here, and are required to do something, every man according to his ability.

Third. The Sabbath school.

Fourth. By personal efforts to lead men to the Savior.

Fifth. By holding up the life of a consistent God as a guide to our own lives.

The widespread interest in the life and martyrdom of this heroic preacher led Editor Senn of the *Deadwood Daily Telegram* to gather what he could of his life story prior to coming to Deadwood. This biographical sketch, as published in the *Telegram* on August 18, 1924, was as follows:

Rev. Henry Weston Smith was born in Ellington, Conn., January 10, 1827.

He was six feet tall, dark complexioned, black hair and eyes, full beard and mustache.

As a youth he was an earnest Christian. At the age of 23 he was licensed as an "exhorter" by the Methodist Church. Later he was ordained as a minister, and held pastorates at several places in Connecticut.

On Oct. 3, 1847, he married Ruth Yeomans of Franklin, Conn. She lived one year after marriage and she and her infant son were buried in the same grave.

In 1857, he married Lydia Ann Joslin of Tolland, Conn. She and three children survived the tragic death of the husband and father.

In 1861, Mr. Smith enlisted in Company H, 52d Massachusetts Infantry. He was in a number of engagements, and after nine months' service was mustered out.

In 1867, he was admitted to the practice of medicine.

In 1867, the family moved to Louisville, Ky. In the meantime he had resumed work as a preacher of the gospel.

Hearing a call to do religious work in the new west, he left in March, 1876, for Cheyenne. After being there a short time he came to the Black Hills, first to Custer City, then to Deadwood. He worked as a miner for a livelihood and preached on the streets. He was held in esteem by many for his self-sacrifice and unpretentious demeanor and upright conduct.

On the morning of August 20, 1876, he preached in Deadwood, then left a note pinned to his cabin door, "Gone to Crook City, back at 2 P.M." On the way there he was murdered supposedly by Indians. His body was found later in the day and brought to Deadwood.

Interment was made in Mount Moriah Cemetery, Deadwood, and a life-size statue of sandstone erected over his grave. This was crumbled badly, being of soft stone. Several years ago an imposing monument was erected on the Deadwood-Spearfish road, near the place of his death.

He had intended bringing his family to Deadwood a few months after arrival. Two years after his death they moved to Texas. In 1882 they returned to Kentucky and in 1885 moved back to Massachusetts, residing in Worcester.

"From Sin to Cinders"
from *Gold, Gals, Guns, Guts*
Bob Lee, Stan Lindstrom,
Wynn Lindstrom, Editors
1976

Momentarily felled by a succession of floods and fires in its early years, Deadwood would rise from the mud and ashes, made more permanent by bricks and mortar, the routing of streams, and the advent of fire departments intended to protect the new structures and the souls they housed.

Deadwood's cataclysm of September 26, 1879, was undoubtedly the product of poor planning, incendiary buildings, no firewalls, and a near-nonexistent response mechanism. Some compared it to the Great Chicago Fire just eight years earlier, which had killed hundreds and leveled four square miles of the Windy City. Indeed, there were parallels, including the overuse of wood in construction, firewood stacked in virtually every building awaiting cool fall nights and the harsh realities of the coming winter, and a lack of a concerted initial response.

Veteran Black Hills newspaperman Bob Lee, aided by assistant editors Wynn and Stan Lindstrom, recounted Deadwood's own great conflagration in their book Gold, Gals, Guns, Guts *produced for the Deadwood-Lead Centennial celebration in 1976. Scouring the archives of Black Hills newspapers and the microfilm of local libraries, the trio provided the best published account of what was then the worst disaster to confront any town in Dakota Territory.*

While some may have been tempted to let the fire's devastation give them cause to depart Deadwood, the gold in the ground caused many more to stay and rebuild. Even when subsequent floods swept away buildings and supplies, the yellow metal held sway. And Lee and his compatriots wrote well of the indomitable pioneer spirit that led those who had suffered great loss to persevere and plan for brighter tomorrows.

Four years of uncontrolled growth went up in smoke in the early morning hours of September 26, 1879, when fire wiped out a major portion of Deadwood Gulch so rapidly that it left the populace of the gold-mining settlement completely stunned. The community would rise, phoenix-like, out of the ashes with a new nickname for Deadwood: "City of Sin and Ashes." The sin had been present from the beginning; the ashes symbolized the burned out passions of the undisciplined gold seekers. The disastrous fire was the gold camp's first major tragedy. Others would follow.

Deadwood holds the record for having the first fire department organization of its kind in the Black Hills. The Pioneer Hook and Ladder Company had been formed in June, 1877, and on its roster appeared the names of 64 Deadwood businessmen. Its equipment included 100 canvas buckets and the running gear of an old wagon fitted up as a hook and ladder truck. In January, 1879, the first hose company was organized but it was disbanded before the fire of September 26 that year.

In the first years of its boisterous existence the numerous houses of "ill repute" that catacombed Main and other narrow streets, marked Deadwood as a sinful town. After the September conflagration the cinders lay thick over most of the business district and up the terraced, residential streets of Forest Hill. Subsequent town and forest fires over the years have added depth to the ashes.

A more modern and beautiful Deadwood emerged from the costly fire that destroyed many hastily and improvised business houses and homes, thus proving a blessing in a satanic, brimstone-and-fire disguise. But to future tourists flocking into Deadwood each year expecting to find a sprawling gold camp like the one depicted in moving pictures, most evidence of the early-day town, including the saloon where Wild Bill Hickok was shot and killed, went up in smoke on that fateful day in 1879.

Early-day accounts vary slightly but generally agree that the fire started in the Empire Bakery which was situated on Sherman Street near where the Adams Museum was later located. It was operated by a Mrs. Ellsner. An overturned kerosene lamp set off the blaze and in minutes it had spread from the frame wooden building to the Jensen and Bliss Hardware Store three doors down the block of tinder-box buildings. Eight kegs of blasting powder in the hardware store exploded with a blast that shook the entire gulch and showered the downtown section with fire and firearms.

Fear-crazed tenants of the upper floors of the business district fled in terror up the steep sides of Deadwood Gulch to safety. The flames spread rapidly to homes stacked like match boxes upon the narrow, terraced streets of Forest Hill.

The *Chicago Tribune* and *Times* devoted four columns to the tragic Black Hills fire. The Deadwood *Black Hills Times* on October 2, 1879, stated that the Chicago paper's "account of our conflagration in the main was correct, but their correspondents evidently exaggerated when they say that a strong wind was blowing at the time. The fact is, not a breeze was in motion at the time the fire broke out and the only air stirring was created by the flames which carried the fire in a northerly direction. Most of the families resided south of the burnt district in South Deadwood, Ingleside and Cleveland. The estimate of our losses is not largely overestimated. It will certainly reach one and one-half million dollars."

"Most destructive fire that ever occurred in the Territory of Dakota destroyed the greater and all the most valuable portion of Deadwood, commercial capital of the Black Hills Mining District," was the way Jesse Brown and A. M. Willard described the catastrophe in their book, *Black Hills Trails.*

The account added that "in the brief time the fire crossed Lee Street, which runs east and west, and was licking up the business houses with their contents; the people seemed paralyzed or half-crazed and hundreds of them climbed the hills on each side with a few valuable possessions, watching their dwellings go up in smoke. The fire passed down Main Street to Gold and Wall Streets and ran on the hill for three blocks, leveling everything. In other directions it extended along Sherman Street until it was checked by small buildings that were

DWOOD AFTER THE GREAT FIRE
T. 26TH 1879

Deadwood suffered a series of floods and fires in its early years. Following
the devastating Great Fire of 1879, merchants and city leaders recon-
structed the town in bricks and mortar. The ravaged town is shown here
in a period postcard following the conflagration. (Photo courtesy of the Adams Museum,
Deadwood, SD)

blown up, saving some residences of excellent design on Ingleside and
the Cleveland Districts." The observer reported 100 business houses
and 75 dwellings were destroyed and estimated the damage at about
three million dollars. A later account listed approximately 300 buildings burned and placed the loss at more than a million dollars.

Annie Tallent, in her book, *The Black Hills, Last Hunting Grounds of the Dakotahs,* gave a stirring account of the fire. After telling of the blasting powder explosion in the hardware store on Sherman Street, she wrote, "in a few minutes the Welch House on Lee Street was ablaze, thence the flames leaped onto Main Street, down which it spread from one inflammable structure to another until the whole of that portion of town from the old courthouse south to Williams Street and to Chinatown on the north was one continuous blaze. Since Deadwood had no perfected water systems for fire, it only stopped at last for lack of material to feed upon."

Mrs. Tallent commented on the fact that "the fire of 1879 was to Deadwood what the fire of 1871 was to Chicago, only the blow fell more heavily on the former in that it was hundreds of miles by wagon train away from its supplies." She also added, "By a singular coincidence a woman was innocently responsible at both disasters." (Mrs. Ellsner's bakery and Mrs. O'Leary's cow.)

The pages of Deadwood's two newspapers, the *Pioneer* and the *Times,* as far back as 1877, revealed a premonition of things to come— a fear in the gulch that fire might be the community's greatest enemy and that means to combat it were nil. On January 2, 1878, the *Times* chronicled an adjourned meeting held at the Bella Union Theatre where Dr. J. H. Harding was appointed chairman and James McPherson secretary. The committee appointed was to ascertain the best location for sinking three wells on Main Street for use in case of fire.

The *Times* reported that on "October 1, 1879, Chief Engineer Richards received a reply from the chief engineer of Chicago's fire department dated September 25, just one day preceding our great pyrotechnic celebration. The letter was written in reply to one written by Richards to the Chicago chief making inquiries about the latest improved hose and other fire equipment."

The September 30, 1879, edition of the *Times* stated that the banks resumed business on that day, the First National in the Chambers C. Davis old Army office and Stebbins, Post and Mund on their old site, having hastily erected a temporary building over their vault. (Bank vaults survived the conflagration without too much damage.) The story continued: "All depositors are 'not grumbling' and deposits up several thousand. All waited patiently with the utmost confidence. Not a syllable of distrust in our banking houses was heard even before the vaults were proven to be secure and contents uninjured. It is without precedent in any country that has had our bitter experience."

The same edition of the *Times* ran columns of loss reports of various business firms. It was surprising how many firms were in Deadwood Gulch only four years after the town's establishment. The newspaper listed 116 firms in one column on Main Street alone. All businessmen expressed determination to rebuild. One item in the midst of business losses stated, "Chinatown, no loss sustained by the heathens. They stole more than they lost in the fire." Another item in the same issue said, "Porter Warner, proprietor of the *Times,* left for Chicago on yesterday's Bismarck coach, and will return with an entire new outfit for the *Times* in a few days."

A column on current conditions of Main Street after the fire listed post-fire activity. For example: "Ben Baer is selling from his fire-proof, D. Holsman is selling his clothes from his fireproof and has a new building started, California George has his chop house running in a tent and will put up a new two-story buildup."

An October 2, 1879, item in the *Times* said, "The heat was so intense during the late fire that the lead bushings on which the host sockets were imbedded in the hydrants of the city water works were all melted out and yesterday Mr. Sacheti was overhauling and repairing them."

Many reports on the fire stated that it was a miracle no deaths were recorded in the conflagration. But a comprehensive story in the Black Hills Pioneer on November 4, 1879, listed one death. The victim was John King, an Englishman known locally as "Casino Jack." The gambler was asleep in his room at the Stone Hotel, believed to be on Lee Street. He was known to be "pretty deaf" and apparently didn't hear the alarm. His death was not verified for several days until workmen found his charred remains when removing debris for rebuilding the hotel on the lot.

Another oddity of the fire was its effect on the canine population of Deadwood. In their fright they virtually stampeded and raced yelping and barking all the way to Crook City before they stopped. A driver of a stagecoach headed for Deadwood said the road was full of canines going at full speed out of the blazing town.

Although only the first of many major fires to plague the timber-lined gulch community, the September 26, 1879, holocaust was the most memorable. Its destructiveness worsened with each re-telling as the old-timers who were there recalled the blazing inferno for their children and grandchildren in later years. Eventually the date of the historic fire was established to identify the real Black Hills pioneers. Only those who were in the Black Hills prior to the fire merited the title; those who came later were tenderfeet. The only difficulty with the test is that the fire also destroyed the official City and County records (to the everlasting sorrow of historians) and documentation of residency prior to Sept. 26 of that fateful year is almost impossible to prove. Nonetheless, the number of "true pioneers" of the region who claimed to have seen the cinders, if not the sin, of Deadwood Gulch circa 1879 staggers the imagination. Perhaps it's just as well that the records did burn. There'd undoubtedly be a lot fewer "pioneers" if they hadn't!

Courage against the Odds

The decade, 1880–1890, was an extension of the turbulent years following the gold rush. It was a time of Indian troubles, mining intrigues, natural disasters, community rivalries, and quirks of human nature. But populations of the Black Hills towns had leveled off. The 1880 census listed 16,486 people in Lawrence, Pennington and Custer counties. Town populations for the three counties listed Anchor City at 291, Central City 1,008, Crook City 100, Custer 271, Deadwood 3,777, Diamond City 30, Elizabethtown 316, Galena 59, Gayville 130, Hayward 38, Lead 1,437, Minneapolis 35, Myersville 103, Pennington

51, Rapid City 292, Rochford 315, Rockerville 321, Sheridan 152, South Bend 209, Spearfish 170, Sturgis 60 and Terraville 775. Thus, Lawrence County was by far the most populated.

The transformation from boomtown mining camp into a stable community was probably difficult for the early settlers. The community leaders were trying to bring some form of law and order into an area still experiencing growing pains. The settlers who wanted to stay and build homes, start businesses, or simply set up tents and work placer claims were contrasted by the "get rich quick" miners and the "get rich any way" train robbers. As the years progressed during the decade, lawlessness gave way to order. Mining proved more difficult than many newcomers had first believed, and the temporary settlers with their dreams of immediate riches moved on. Gradually, a permanent core of settlers stabilized the community.

The science of medicine during the 1880's was still in its infancy, but progress in modernization of mining camp medical facilities was being noted in Deadwood. It was in a March 1883 issue of the *Black Hills Daily Times* that an editorial appeared suggesting that a new County Hospital and Poor Farm be constructed near Deadwood to care for the poor and needy. The proposal was defeated in a county election because the public did not want higher taxes to pay for the project. So nothing was done.

Two years later, in 1885, a grand jury was called to investigate the County Hospital. At the time of the inquiry, 13 patients were hospitalized in the facility. The grand jury found crowded sleeping conditions, ten patients in one small room, poor ventilation, dirty bedclothes and filthy rooms. The patients suffering from broken bones or similar ailments were sleeping in the same room with those afflicted by tuberculosis. Interestingly, the kitchen and dining areas were clean. The grand jury recommended that a more suitable place be found for the care of the county poor. Changes had to be made, Dr. D. K. Dickinson, a former Homestake doctor, was appointed to replace Dr. Z. S. McKowan as the County Physician and gradually the conditions at the county hospital were brought up to acceptable standards.

Progress in modernization of the Homestake Hospital occurred in 1886 when a two-story building was erected. The doctors' offices were located on the first floor and the patients' rooms on the second. This building served the Homestake miners and their families until it was rebuilt during the next century.

The Deadwood hospital, which provided medical care for the community as a whole rather than just the miners, was converted into a school for boys by Father Peter Rosen, a local Catholic missionary, following the flood of 1883. The school, St. Edward's Academy, was reopened under the supervision of the Sisters of the Holy Cross.

Although many physicians did the best they could under the circumstances, on many occasions a patient's ailment would be incorrectly diagnosed or a patient might be given the wrong prescription. The *Black Hills Daily Times,* realizing medicine was a relatively new science, gave its support to the area doctors even though many unintentional deaths occurred under a physician's care. Doctors Dickinson and Rogers amputated the leg of Richard Freudenberg who had been injured in a ranch accident. The patient died and Freudenberg's father felt that his son's death was caused by the neglect of the doctors while his son was hospitalized. Dr. Dickinson said his duty had been performed in the case and no charges of malpractice were brought against him. But malpractice suits were not uncommon in the county. The *Black Hills Daily Times* mentions that three civil suits were brought against a prominent physician, but the civil actions were later dropped and the doctor continued to serve the community. Seldom was a doctor ever found to be incompetent. Doctors were too rare and valuable to lose.

Considering the turbulent period in which the early doctors worked and their limited knowledge of medicine, the first physicians performed their duties admirably. The pioneer doctors were called upon at all hours to deliver babies, perform surgery, and visit patients. Many of their first surgical attempts proved successful. A record was made in the *Black Hills Daily Times* of a delicate operation successfully conducted by Dr. Dickinson on the arm of a man who had been injured in a sawmill accident. Numerous cases of the amputation of human limbs due to frostbite were handled expertly by Doctors Dickinson, Freeman, and McKowan. As the decade 1880–1890 progressed, the pioneer doctors in the county had established themselves as first rate humanitarians and conscientious physicians.

The newspapers of the period provide insight into the 1880–1890 era of transformation. The *Black Hills Daily Times* examined the problems and voiced the hopes of a community attempting to mature during a decade of unrest. But the unrest was a particularly complicated problem. An item for the date March 10, 1880, reads: "A gold bullion robbery occurred at Sidney, Nebraska. The treasure in the form of gold bricks was an express shipment from the mines in the Lead and Deadwood gulches. One $1,000 brick was identified as coming from the Esmerelda Mine. The robbery was believed to have been planned in advance. A posse later captured the robbers."

Articles appeared frequently in the old newspapers complaining of the lawlessness and violence. Editorials would demand more law enforcement and yet crime continued. Occasionally, renegade Indians and-or whites intensified criminal activities. In May of 1880, mention is made of a reputed Indian raid in the Redwater and Belle Fourche valleys. A number of horses and cattle were reported taken. The question was whether whites or Indians were responsible.

The exploits of highwaymen and bandits were often reported. An item for July 25, 1880, reads: "Road agents Jack Campbell and Big Nose George were rounded up after holding up the stage from Sidney, Nebraska." Even embezzlers were not uncommon in Deadwood Gulch. In the September 8 issue, it was written that R. O. Adams, convicted ex-postmaster of Deadwood, was captured at Fort Sully by two soldiers. He had absconded with post office funds.

Frequently, warnings would appear in the early newspapers urging future prospectors from the East to be prepared to work hard to find mineral riches since "gold does not grow on trees." Inevitably, prospectors would become disappointed and frustrated. Even though they worked hard, these early day miners sometimes would have little to show for their toil. Disappointment could lead to conflicts with other miners over claims or frustrated miners would turn to illegal means to find the end of the rainbow.

Two cases tried in U.S. District Court at Deadwood during the 1880's have proved the basis for important decisions in similar cases since that time. One involved mining rights and the other the prosecution of Indians for crimes on the reservation.

Galena, with a vivid history which rivals that of any other gold or mining town in the Black Hills, was the site of the mining law controversy. Early prospectors in search of gold, discovered the silver bearing ore in the deep gulches surrounded by high mountains. In two of the claims located was found the vein of galena which gave the town its name.

These claims, the Florence and the Sitting Bull, were centered in the dispute which was settled when the court held that a claim followed the vein of ore horizontally rather than vertically.

Here is the story vouched for by old-timers of Galena and Deadwood, court records, accounts in newspapers at the time and from mining law books.

Colonel J. H. Davey, a picturesque figure, wearing the wide hat, flowing tie, trousers stuffed into high boots costume of the period, arrived in the Black Hills from the East in the early 1880's. An expert in the treatment of white metal, he acquired an interest in the Florence mine at Galena, later buying it with some other properties. He went in for extensive development, erecting a completely equipped, ten-stamp mill, said to be the first of its kind in the Black Hills.

It cost about $80 a ton to haul the ore from Galena to Fort Pierre by bull train so Davey needed to operate at full tilt.

Pat Duggan owned the Silver Terra and Richmond properties next to Davey's claims. Duggan and Davey got into an argument over the dip of the ore vein. Duggan accused Davey of dipping into the ore vein on his property and declared that he had the right to follow the vein wherever it led, and that Davey had no right to go over the endline of the claim. Davey contended that he was entitled to follow the vein to its apex, whether the apex was on his claim or some other. In short it must be decided whether the vein was horizontal or vertical.

The fiery colonel put his men to work on the Silver Terra end of the Sitting Bull claim and they got out the ore as rapidly as possible, filling in the stopes with waste as fast as the ore was taken out. He threw up a bulwark underground and placed an armed guard between the lines. Although the question never has been settled satisfactorily, it is certain that by means of this tactic, Davey was able to extract most of the ore before Duggan could tunnel into his claim from the top and drift toward the ore vein.

Quarrels were inevitable. Davey's son, Frank, and Billy Thatcher, [on the] lookout for the Sitting Bull, rode to the Galena Post Office where they met Patrick Gorman, a Duggan man. In the argument that followed, Gorman was killed. The coroner's jury declared that though Gorman carried a gun, he was killed by a bullet from Thatcher's gun. Davey's lawyers cleared Thatcher, claiming self defense and he left the country never to be heard of again.

Duggan's next move was to close all the properties by injunction and bring suit against Davey for damages. The case dragged along for months in the United States District Court of the Territory of Dakota, Judge J. H. Church on the bench. The hearing, in the summer of 1883, took 65 days. The entire court made a trip to Galena to look over the property. One hundred witnesses were examined and the testimony covered 7,000 pages. Finally the jury arrived at a verdict for the plaintiff, Duggan. Davey's lawyers appealed to the Supreme Court of the Territory. The trial court judgment was sustained but before the decision was handed down Davey had exhausted his funds and left the Black Hills.

The legal fight killed the town although it had a brief revival in 1897 when the price of silver was high.

The other now-famous decision involved Crow Dog, who was found guilty of killing the famous Spotted Tail at the Brule Sioux Agency in August, 1881. Crow Dog was tried at Deadwood and sentenced to be executed January 14, 1884.

A Deadwood lawyer, A. J. Plowman, who represented Crow Dog at the trial, contended that no offense was committed under the existing law because both the defendant and the victim were Indians.

Crow Dog, of course, was destitute and no arrangements were available in federal courts at that time for the payment of an attorney to defend him. However, Plowman was able in some manner to secure the attention of the United States Congress and an appropriation was made in the Act of March 3, 1883, to advance the sum of $1,000 to cover the costs of taking the case to the United States Supreme Court to test this question of jurisdiction. The high court held that the federal court was without jurisdiction and ordered Crow Dog released.

The discovery by this decision of the highest court in the land [that] there was no law forbidding the killing of one Indian by another Indian in Indian territory caused quite a concern in the country. As a result Congress hastened to pass the Act which forbids all Indians in Indian country from committing the crimes enumerated against other Indians, which is the basis of the prosecution of Indians in federal court today.

Being first the hub of the mining in the Northern Black Hills when gold was first discovered, and later designated as the county seat, Deadwood has always been the center for legal actions and lawyers. In fact, in 1881 a pamphlet published by the Deadwood Board of Trade listed a greater number of attorneys than the town has seen recently for some period of time. They included the following lawyers and firms:

Burns, John H.	Caulfield & Carey
Clagett & Dixon	Chadwick, W. L.
Choteau & Bowman	Corson & Thomas
Cranston, John	Frawley, Henry
Frank, A. E.	Gaffy, Lorin E.
Graham, N. J.	Graham, F. C.
Harvey & Gantt	Houghton, Dick

Haydon & Alien	Hastie, A.W.
Kingsley, William C.	Kohn, Edward
Liverman, Moses	Martin, Eben W.
McLaughlin & Steele	Miller & McGinnis
McGinnis, John	Moody, Gideon C.
Mullaly, J. S.	Offenbacher, J.V.
Parker, William H.	Potter, Daniel
Plowman, A. J.	Romans, S.P.
Smalley, E.H.	Scofield, G.B.
Racy & Hamilton	Van Cise & Wilson
Watson, J.F.	Wetmore, E.A.
Washabaugh, F.J.	Young, J.M.

In September, 1882, President Garfield appointed Judge William E. Church to the U.S. District Court where he served until 1886 when he was succeeded by Judge Charles M. Thomas, named by the Cleveland administration, who presided until the end of the Territorial Courts in 1889. That year when South Dakota became a state, Judge Thomas was elected to the bench of the Eighth Judicial District, which consisted of Lawrence, Butte and Meade counties.

More than any other period, this was the time when the law reflected the spirit of its clientele, and consequently was relatively loose and freewheeling. Not yet a state, the Attorney Association, such as it was, exercised little influence over its practitioners, who all carried advertisements in the local newspapers touting their legal expertise in areas such as mining and property rights. This advertising was, of course, a practice that was later banned by the bar association when the attorneys decided that they should not be hawking their professional capacities (or incapacities) in public.

Many of the lawyers first came to the Hills for the same reason as others . . . to pan for gold and strike it rich. Those who didn't, found that the law business was a tricky one that did not readily supply them with a living source of income. The practice of law, like the times, was precarious. In the *Black Hills Trails* by Jesse Brown there is recounted the early experience of a well-known Lead attorney by the name of Tom Harvey. This pioneer lawyer first settled in Custer during the original rush, more to seek gold than to practice law. Drifting up to Deadwood, he was fortunate, as his story goes, to be engaged by a bank there for some legal work. Upon the successful completion of the work, he was paid in six new ten-dollar bills. Satisfied with his days work and his fee, he bedded down in the IXL Hotel for a good night's sleep only to awake in the morning to find his clothes scattered and his money gone. With not another cent to his name, he borrowed some money for a fare to Custer on the stage that was leaving later that afternoon. While waiting for that vehicle, he was hailed by a fellow who was being hauled off to jail by the local sheriff.

The fellow identified himself as Jack Rhodes, a person Harvey had successfully defended in Cheyenne some time before. Rhodes pleaded with Harvey to defend him once again. He was reluctant but stated that he would do so if Rhodes paid him a $100 retainer. Whereupon, Rhodes pulled out a huge wad of bills and promptly pealed off the money. Included in the retainer were six new ten dollar bills, the very bills that had been stolen from Harvey the night before. Taking Rhodes aside, Harvey told him in no uncertain terms that he was a no-good reprobate and that if he didn't turn over all of the money stolen from all of the guests at the hotel the previous night, he would really be in trouble. Surprised, Rhodes gave Harvey all of the rest of his ill-gotten money, whereupon Harvey marched him to the judge where charges were dropped, money returned and case completed. Harvey had matters settled quickly enough to be able to board the Custer stage and be gone.

During this violent era, murders were common. In a December issue, it was reported that James Layton Gilane was publicly hanged for homicide. An article appeared in the paper deploring the barbaric use of capital punishment. Lynchings also occurred. The old paper reports that on August 24, 1885, Dr. V. P. Lynch was assassinated in Sturgis by Corporal Ross Hallon of Fort Meade who was, in turn, lynched by an angry mob.

Fires and natural disasters occurred with disturbing frequency in the Deadwood gulches and surrounding region during the 1880's. The *Black Hills Daily Times* reports that after the fire of 1879, 50 new buildings were in the course of construction. A positive outlook for the Hills was forecast. However, fire bugs were cause for alarm up and down the gulch in Lead, Central City and Deadwood. Such people were "too mean to live in any community," the local newspaper stated.

In 1881, a fire destroyed a drug store and a variety shop on Deadwood's Lee Street. Fire departments from Lead, Deadwood and Central City kept the fire from spreading. The *Black Hills Daily Times* mentions that many comments came from the people on the sidelines, but little help was forthcoming from them. A better system of fire alarm was necessary and a bell was installed on the Congregational Church.

On a day in 1881 when the air was heavy and sultry, a cyclone, accompanied by torrents of rain and hail, swept down City Creek as far as McGovern Hill and turned back up City Creek. One woman was killed and several people were injured. Houses were flattened and people took refuge in mine tunnels. "This destroying force appeared like a gigantic column a thousand feet high and one hundred feet in diameter," exclaimed the *Times*. A tremendous flood occurred on May 16, 1883, and hailstorms of huge proportions devastated 20,000 acres of farmland in Butte and Lawrence counties the next year. Another hailstorm in 1884 despoiled 50,000 acres. The hail was alleged to be as big as a man's fist. Crops were wiped clean and the agricultural loss was set at $200,000.

The night of March 10, 1883, near Brownsville in Elk Creek Valley, 11 men died in a fire. Buried in a mass grave at Mount Moriah Cemetery in Deadwood on March 13, 1883, were Albert Tunnicliff, Raisha C. Rice, James Chalmers, Samuel Haines, Fred D. Peters, Thomas Finless, Charles Hammontree, Peter Hanson, Louis Hanson, Harvey Woods and W. H. Andrews. The men were employed by Hood and Scott at a nearby lumber mill. They were sleeping in the second story of a rough boarding house, provided by the company, when the fire started, presumably in the kitchen, and sent clouds of smoke into the sleeping quarters. Some of the men were overcome by the smoke and tried to escape. Some who got out, for some reason, went back into the building and they too were overcome by smoke and died. Four other men were badly burned but escaped. Little was known of the men whose ages ranged from 22 to 50 years. Relatives of Rice and Tunnicliff erected monuments to them at the cemetery.

Best reported among the natural disasters of the 1880's was the devastating flood of May 16, 1883, that brought Deadwood to the edge of extinction for the second time. The community had suffered its first flood damage in the spring of 1878 when a late season snowstorm piled huge drifts in the gullies and gulches of the mining camp. A sudden downpour of rain melted the snow and sent Deadwood and Whitewood Creeks over their banks, seriously undermining buildings along their edges. Nevertheless, when the waters receded, building continued along the two streams that yearly merged forces in the center of town. The populace was to pay a terrible price for its neglect of the obvious threat.

Conditions in the spring of 1883 were identical to those that had caused the 1878 flood, but this time the damage was far more extensive. Big snows set the stage in mid-May and the heavy rains that followed forced the destructive flood waters into motion. Debris came cascading down every littered gulch and smashed into the Lee Street bridge. Soon the flood waters flowed over and around the bridge and many buildings were washed away. It was estimated the rampaging waters caused over $300,000 in damage and a number of lives were lost.

"The Great Flood," as it became known, was thoroughly reported in the May 18 edition of the *Black Hills Daily Times,* two days after the deluge. It gave this account of the disaster:

On Wednesday noon, the 16th, the barometer took a downward tumble, and it kept going down, down, until a lower point than ever before had been known was reached. Yesterday afternoon (16th) it commenced raining, a steady pouring down rain, that increased in volume with time. The snow that had been lingering in the lap of spring, on the mountain tops, soon yielded to the softening embrace and came rushing down, in rivulets at first, then in torrents. As the stream began to swell, the mayor and city marshal were to be seen with such force as they could procure, clearing out the channel that was clogged up with buildings, bridges and floating debris. At 4 o'clock in the afternoon Dan Rathbun telephoned from Ten Mile ranch that the snow was all leaving the mountains, water was belly deep to a horse everywhere, and to look out for a big flood.

Soon after this Sam Cushman's building, and the Oyster Bay, on Lee street, began settling, and the citizens then realized that they were in danger. The houses were emptied of their contents, fire companies called out, hose attached to hydrants, and with water coming from the clouds in torrents, the Cushman building was saturated with coal oil and fired.

Lee street was thronged with men rushing in every direction, doing everything they could, which was nothing. As a section of firemen were running across the creek in front of the Oyster Bay, the sidewalk went down, carrying James Northey, a Lead City fireman, and Will Warner (now of the Whitewood Sentinel) with it. At that point the water was twelve feet deep, and running with the velocity of a cannon ball, through and under the bridge and between the innumerable posts that were planted everywhere in the creek. Hundreds of men witnessed their entanglement, and a hundred hearts ceased to beat. It seemed that no man could go thro' the maelstrom and live, but in a few moments they came up below the bridge, swimming like ducks (mallards), and very soon landed all right. Northey lost his hat, was slightly cut on the head. Warner had a damaged leg.

Late in the afternoon the water broke out from the channel at Cleveland and came down through Sherman Street deep enough for a steamboat to float. After night set in all was excitement and confusion. Men and women running in every direction, each trying to do something for their own or the community's good. Back of Star & Bullock's, on Sherman street, the chattels and effects of the girls were being removed from the buildings; pianos, with men and women carrying them, could be seen wading through water up to their knees; firemen detailed for special duty could be seen all along the stream.

Ben Garr, a fireman, at the H. and L. Co. house on Sherman street, in attempting to save the house went down with it into the flood, but by pluck, perseverance and luck, landed not far from Harry Damon's, alive, but nearly gone.

At 10 p.m. William Henley telephoned from Gayville to the Times that within an hour Bobtail had increased in volume four fold, Deadwood Creek a fourth and had only commenced to rise, the road washed away and John Alien's dam gone. At this hour a Times man went on to Deadwood street and found three feet of water in Patsy Boliver's house, and neighbors carrying out the traps; Tom Manning's livery barn from which he had at an earlier hour removed the horses and carriages, afloat, bobbing around until it brought up against the bridge, and at this point he saw Fred Fredericks of the Vienna bakery tackle it with an axe. He stood up like a hero and pounded holes in the siding; said he would make it come down and go under the bridge.

Hurrying around to Lee street he was just in time to see the Oyster Bay rear up behind, groan and disappear in the flood, and as the debris went down stream it was for a moment resisted by the H.&L. house that stood on stilts, but it soon succumbed and went out. It was here that Ben Garr went in. This house had previously been fired . . . No one who saw him fall in ever expected to see his lifeless remains, but strange as it may seem, with a tenacity born of desperation, he made a brave fight for his family and his life, coming ashore at the Northwestern company's barn, with a badly contused head and an exhausted body. Harris Franklin's stable on Sherman street quietly arose and quietly sailed down stream, as did Jacoby's marble shop and Butler's shop on Lee street.

Merchants on Main street were busy that night moving goods from the basements. The bridges on Lee, Deadwood, Wall and Pine

*streets went off and all communications with South Deadwood
was cut off. In the way of incidents the record shows that Sam
Cushman, with a spirit that has always actuated him, seeing that
his building on Lee street if left standing would endanger the
whole city, requested Mayor Steele to have it burned. Frank Ickes
was standing on the bank of the stream; it caved in; Frank caved
with it, and but for a colored man who was near at hand and
yanked him out, would have been drowned.*

*At 2 o'clock when going to press, Deadwood street was being
cut away at a fearful rate, the current making for the Vienna
building on Lee street. At 3 o'clock a.m. the danger was so immi-
nent that the fire bell was rung to call the people to the rescue.*

In the issue of the *Times* for May 19, the flood report continued.

*The city water right; continuation of the doleful story of the
destruction of Deadwood; the new high school has disappeared
in the waters; the Methodist church has gone to join the general
wreck and ruin; a wide swath cut zig-zag through the heart of
the city; Chandler, the toll-gate man, his wife and hired man
gone; the water going down.*

*. . . Sherman street below the Pioneer office two doors has
been taken out, all of Lee street up to Headquarters building
gone, all buildings on Bull Flats are gone and an apparent clean
sweep made through to Cleveland. The $12,000 school house
with furniture, and the Methodist church are no more. So immi-
nent is the danger to Main street that all the merchants on the
east side have removed their goods to places of safety. Every con-
ceivable article and animal were seen passing through the city
on the debris of houses from up-gulch, cats, dogs, chickens, hogs,
horses and cattle, pianos, organs, wagons, buggies, stages and a
hearse on their way to the sea.*

*An inch cable was thrown across the gulch, made taut, and
in a chair suspended thereto communication has been established with the other side of the creek. The water main that supplies South Deadwood with water was broken where it crossed
the gulch. This deprived them of water and when at noon a fire*

was seen to be raging in Christie's saloon, opposite the court
house, a good many of our people became discouraged. The roof
of the court house, caught fire and for a time it seemed from this
side of the gulch that everything must go, but the heroic exertions
of a few men who had nothing to fight fire with but water carried
in buckets, it was extinguished and the fire kept from spreading.

In all probability they would not have succeeded had it
not been for the encouragement they received from a hundred
or more able bodied, lazy loafers, who sat on the hillside above
them and never raised a hand.

Dr. Myres and Frank Peck who were mourned as lost, have
turned up, the Dr. spent the night on Hebrew Hill astride a
stump. G. W. Chandler, wife and hired man were seen to set
down to dinner, and a moment afterwards, the house and
contents went into the flood and disappeared. All of them are
known to have found a watery grave. Sam Cushman's safe
weighing 800 lbs. has gone, two other large safes are also miss-
ing, one of which belonged to the Times, *reported loaded with*
Golden Eagle stock, is no more. At 9:30 Mrs. Chandler's body
was found below Harry Damon's.

In conclusion, we will add that the remains of Chandler
were found soon afterwards and later the body of the hired man,
Gustaf Halhusen. The Pioneer *issued no paper for several days*
and the first anyone knew of its being alive, was when Keller
Kurts appeared on the streets asking for subscriptions to a mam-
moth sheet that would be issued in a few days with every par-
ticular of the flood, damage to property, etc. It was at the time
designated as the "sublimity of gall."

During the 1880's, the *Black Hills Daily Times* also carried stories
about the mines, the Board of Trade happenings, religious news, the
fight for statehood, social activities, and the "Fire Laddies," who were
highly politically oriented. The railroad extension into Deadwood was
a favorite topic. News about the several lodges, including the Masons,
Knights of Pythias, IOOF, Knights Templar and G.A.R. frequently
appeared in the papers.

Many community social events were organized during the 1880's. In September of 1881, the second annual Black Hills Fair was held at the Park Association Grounds. Horse races with $6,000 in premiums, a drill by U.S. soldiers, baseball games and wheelbarrow races were some of the events. Also agricultural and mining exhibits were shown. Plays, circuses and operas were also provided for the enjoyment of the public throughout the decade. However, the greatest celebration of the year was the Fourth of July.

The rivalry, bordering hostility, between Lead and Deadwood was apparent in the early paper. The rivalry entered into everything from sports to economics. Prior to the Fourth of July 1882, a heated controversy ensued over which town should stage the festivities, Lead or Deadwood. No compromise was found, and little celebrating occurred.

Politics was another sensitive subject in the Lead-Deadwood communities. During the aldermanic elections of May 1882, great interest was shown by two local political factions, the Solid Six and the Fireman's Citizen Ticket. In the election of May 2, the Fireman's ticket headed by Kirk G. Phillips, won every ward. The proposition of building a new jail and a poor farm for the county was soundly defeated in the election. The public did not want the increased tax burden.

Life in the 1880's in the Lead-Deadwood gulches provided a variety of experiences: some humorous, many frightening and a few tragic. The ability of the first settlers to establish a growing community despite numerous obstacles is a tribute to their pioneer spirit.

"Deadwood—A Modern Sodom Needs Another Renovation" from *Senn's Forum* / Adams Museum

Edward L. Senn

December 1938

Wait long enough, and civilization will arrive, even in America's back-country. In its early years, Deadwood earned a reputation as a wild town with a wicked streak, a place that could never be tamed.

Some say you could find an illegal poker game being played in Deadwood twenty-four hours a day for the better part of a century. Chinese operated opium dens in the Badlands. Prohibition barely slowed the town down, courtesy of subterranean speakeasies. A couple stories overhead, close cribs offered creature comforts for those with a poke. These brothels operated unfettered until federal agents finally closed them down in a 1980 raid. Since then, old-timers say the hunting season has never been the same.

Given the extreme wealth created by Black Hills gold mines, and the bustling commercial enterprises and attendant churches that followed, it was inevitable that the town of Deadwood would eventually gain some semblance of respectability. Periodic calls to "clean it up!" began early with the ranting of Preacher Smith in dirty Deadwood Gulch of the 1870s, then echoed down the long, dry canyon of Prohibition in the 1920s. But Deadwood's seedier side seemingly never died. Nor did those who apparently had adopted among their life missions a calling to keep cleaning it up.

In the midst of a Great Depression that affected agrarian states such as South Dakota with an intensity reserved for few others, Senn's Forum provided fodder for the masses. In 1938, the newspaper called for the strict enforcement of statutes governing bawdy houses, bowling alleys, and bars. These places of disrepute, Senn's feared, were dealing Deadwood the worst hand—a reputation among easterners as a wide-open spot.

"There is still a west and this is its final stand," the tabloid declared. As an early-day diatribe, the following account from Senn's Forum *may be among the best researched you'll encounter—keenly putting its author in frequent proximity to the same venues he seeks to malign, deep in the dark underbelly of a "modern Sodom."*

All who read this article are sufficiently familiar with the Biblical story of ancient Sodom and Gomorrah to understand application of the term "A Modern Sodom" to Deadwood. It is generally admitted, even by present day apologists for "dear, delightful, devilish Deadwood," that in the first years of its existence it was a good reproduction of ancient Sodom. But this article does not speak of the Deadwood of 1876. It tells of the Deadwood of 1938.

There was little improvement in conditions between 1876 and 1910, with lawless elements dominating the city, and vice rampant. During the 15 years following 1910 a vigorous fight was waged, and when W. E. Adams completed his last term as Mayor in 1925, it could truthfully be said that Deadwood was then as law-abiding and free of vice resorts as any other city of its size in the state. Thereafter there was a gradual letting down of obstructions, with spasmodic "clean-ups" until, under the present "wide-open" admin-istration, "the sky is the limit." It no longer is necessary to wait for the annual "Days of '76 Celebration," to see reproduction of condi-tions prevailing in 1876. They can now be seen any day or night by anyone who has the price to pay for the experience and alleged entertainment. In support of such assertions the following bill of particulars is presented:

The intoxicating liquor traffic is licensed in Deadwood as in many other cities in South Dakota. But there is a difference; in other cities and towns there is at least some pretense at observance of the so-called "restrictive features" of the license law, which prohibit: sale to minors and habitual drunkards, after closing hours, on Sundays; any window obstructions "which interfere with a view from the street"; any "game of skill or chance, or dancing or athletic contest or other form of amusement of recreation"; any "slot machine or other like devices." Minors are wholly forbidden to enter such places unless accompanied by parent or guardian. "No license of any class shall permit any intoxicated person to enter his premises or to become intoxicated thereon or therein."

From frequent inspection of the four "on sale" saloons of Deadwood from the outside and occasional inspections from within, it appears that most of these restrictive features are violated by all of them. All open and close when they please, remain open on Sundays and holidays, permit of free entrance of minors, sell liquor indiscriminately to all who have the price, tolerate drunkenness, and on special occasions are bedlams of howling, drunken mobs, nearly half of them women. All of them have music or other entertainment features. All of them have gambling halls in the rear with no obstruction to entering, or at most swinging bars or doors wide open. Two of them have "night clubs" attached upstairs, with stairway from saloon, which on special occasions rival the drunken debauchery of the "Barbary Coast" in San Francisco; and one of them has a wholly enclosed "cocktail lounge" (what a very appropriate name), despite a provision in the law that there shall be no booth or other enclosure in which the occupants are not "within full view of every other occupant in the room" in which the liquor is sold; and one of them has a large café closely connected with wide open entrance from the saloon. All of them also have high-point beer licenses.

In addition to the foregoing there are nine places with "off sale" licenses which confer the privilege of selling hard liquors in sealed containers, which the law says should not be, but which frequently are opened on the premises. Most of these also have high-point beer licenses, and some of them sell hard liquors by the drink.

In addition to these thirteen places selling hard liquors and, with one exception, all high-point beer, there are eleven exclusive beer licenses. Most of such licenses are held by resorts on lower Main Street, which are in fact bawdy house speak-easies. That they are hard liquor speak-easies is evidenced by the fact that they have federal permits for the sale of such liquors, preferring to pay the $25 per year tax to the federal government to obtain immunity from interference by federal revenue officers. There is no local interference with these joints, and no effort to enforce the hard liquor laws by city, county or state officers. While Sioux Falls and some other cities have had some spasmodic efforts by state officers to enforce the liquor laws during

Despite laws to the contrary, for more than a century a visitor to Deadwood could play poker, drink liquor, or spend time with an "upstairs girl" twenty-four hours a day, seven days a week. (Photo courtesy of the Adams Museum, Deadwood, SD)

the past two years, Deadwood appears to have been wholly immune from any such "interference with business." The last "clean-up" was under the Berry administration, two and one-half years ago.

In addition to the 24 places in which intoxication liquors may be purchased, Deadwood has, for entertainment of citizens and visitors, six well-equipped gambling resorts, which are as open and accessible as other places of business, day and night, so long as the supply of suckers holds out. As stated, four of these gambling resorts are closely connected with the four "on sale" saloons. There are also two others run in connection with places which have "off sale" and high-point beer licenses. In these six gambling joints a wide variety of entertainment is offered, including roulette, craps, faro, Black Jack, poker and other games with which this writer is not familiar.

Then there are the bawdy house resorts, eight or ten of them, each having three to five inmates, with booze, dancing and other "entertainment."

Probably some will think, even in Deadwood, that the foregoing is exaggerated. Not so. It is based mostly on repeated personal observation and the remainder on information obtained from reliable informants who are in position to know. Such is Deadwood's reputation, far and wide. That it has such reputation is known to the businessmen of Deadwood, and many of them glory in it. In a bulletin on "Civic News" published by the Deadwood Chamber of Commerce, dated September 26, 1938, is given an item which confirms the foregoing description of conditions. It is an "Excerpt from the Boston Transcript, July 16, 1938," which reads as follows:

Many easterners revel in Deadwood. Some aver that Broadway could learn a lot from this city. Sheriff Hickok has long since passed to his reward, but the prevailing western atmosphere attests to the fact that Deadwood is a misnomer for that "wide open" spot. The east has no counterpart for it. There is still a west and this is its final stand.

Read that again and read between the lines. The writer intended to convey that even Broadway, with its notorious wickedness, could take lessons along that line from Deadwood. The Transcript writer evidently was here early in the summer. Had he been here during the "Days of '76" celebration in August, he would have written less circumspectly. This writer toured old Clark Street in Chicago and "The Levee" in St. Louis at the zenith of their fame for vice and lawlessness nearly fifty years ago. They also could have "learned a lot" from the Deadwood of 1938.

But, some one may say, "Haven't you officers of the law in Deadwood?" Sure! Half a dozen city and county officers who took oath to "uphold the laws" of this city and state. They do try to enforce the laws against murder, grand larceny, public rioting, auto speeding (sometimes), and out of town drunks who can pay a fine. But when it comes to enforcing laws against gambling, prostitution and illegal sale of liquor, they appear to be blind, deaf and dumb. They are average good citizens, but apparently are "hog-tied" by those who make appointments and control administrative officers. They have families to support and must obey orders.

But haven't you any church organizations and ministers in Deadwood? Sure! We're not all heathen. There are half a dozen organizations with resident pastors, all "faithful workers," and most of them have their own church buildings. Several hundred people go to church on Sunday—nearly as many as go to the saloons and dives on Saturday night. But the ministers are busy "sowing good seed" around the edges of this big field of thistles, that they apparently are oblivious to the necessity for plowing up the weeds preparatory to sowing.

But haven't you good women in Deadwood? Sure! Hundreds of them who don't go to the saloons, or even the night clubs. But most of them are so busy with their Ladies Aids, and Missionary Societies, and numerous Clubs, and bridge parties, and golf and other social engagements, that they haven't much time left to give to remedying the conditions on lower Main Street which are ruining many of our youth and sending out a stream of pollution which extends far beyond the borders of this city and state. Every year scores of young men and women come to Deadwood who are not as clean morally or physically when they leave as when they came.

Why are the good people, who are in a majority even in Deadwood, so indifferent to these frightful conditions? There are several reasons. One is the apparently almost unanimous sentiment of the business interests of the city in favor of "wide open" conditions; another is lack of a newspaper or other means of publicity which will expose the conditions; possibly another is a lack of knowledge by many of the full extent to which vice and lawlessness have entered the city following return of the legalized liquor traffic.

With the first of these reasons the writer can do little directly; but the other two will be remedied by sending copies of this paper to hundreds of Deadwood men and women who should be much concerned over the conditions and willing to take active steps to remedy them. There is one platform on which all good citizens of Deadwood should be willing to stand, regardless of views on prohibition and other methods of dealing with the intoxicating liquor traffic, and that is: so long as the license system is in vogue, liquor dealers should be required to comply strictly with all restrictive features of the law; and no licenses should be issued to bawdy houses, or to bowling alleys or other places of recreation where young people congregate.

When similar conditions were exposed thirty years ago, the exposer was accused of "disloyalty," and "hurting business," and "befouling his own nest." Even from the pulpit he was condemned for "contaminating the atmosphere by stirring up the foul cesspools of vice." It is probable that similar condemnation will now come from those who place their own financial interests above the moral welfare of the community. But it is hoped that this exposure will again bring to the city relief from intolerable conditions.

(Note: The *Forum* is not printed in Deadwood. Shortly before going to press word was received by the printer from the publisher that the city council of Deadwood, in special session the evening previous, had "for various reasons" rejected nine applications for "off sale" package liquor licenses and granted only three. With forms made up, further information and comment on this action by the editor must be deferred until next issue.)

PART II

WILD BILL HICKOK AND CALAMITY JANE

———————————

A town is sometimes characterized by those who inhabit it, however briefly. Such is the case with Deadwood, where the lingering legacy of Wild Bill Hickok and Calamity Jane remains more than 130 years after they first arrived in this lawless land.

Only in the past few decades have researchers come to grips with the realities of these two Western legends, documenting the number of men Wild Bill actually gunned down, and surmising that Calamity Jane may well have been the Paris Hilton of her day—famous for simply being famous. But, we can no more ignore the contributions these two characters had on the lasting mystique of Deadwood than we can dismiss the profound impact that the discovery of gold had on the Black Hills.

In the following excerpts, taken from several of the most thorough researchers and biographers to ever explore the topic, we get a sense of the man dubbed the Prince of Pistoleers and the female often described as the One-Woman Cyclone.

"Wild Bill's Demise"
from *They Called Him Wild Bill: The Life and Adventures of James Butler Hickok*
Joseph G. Rosa
1974

Joseph G. Rosa has made his lifelong pursuit the American West, from the firearms that helped tame it and the people who helped populate it, to the legends and lore that linger like wood smoke long after the fire has died.

What, perhaps, is even more remarkable is that Rosa is an Englishman, separated from his subject by a couple thousand miles of ocean and land. A resident of Ruislip, Middlesex, England, Rosa has served as an officer in the English Westerners' Society. His affinity for the American West is best evidenced in his first major book on Wild Bill, which he dedicated to the late Gary Cooper (1901–1961), "whose portrayal of Wild Bill Hickok in The Plainsman *inspired the research that led to this book."*

Rosa has authored many books about the American West, including the definitive 1996 Wild Bill *biography,* Wild Bill Hickok: The Man and His Myth, The Gunfighter: Man or Myth?, Alias Jack McCall, Guns of the American West, Colt Revolvers and the Tower of London, *and* Men and Weapons on the Frontier, 1840–1900, *as well as numerous articles on Western subjects and antique firearms for both English and American journals.*

Rosa is at his best when he is discounting myths and wending his way down the path to their origins. He exposes deliberate lies, sheds light on gross exaggerations, and has a confirmed tendency to set the record straight. But, in so doing, Rosa doesn't lessen the lore or abandon the telling. Rather, for the reader he rolls the myths over in his mind, savoring then dissecting them for a better understanding of how they came to glorify the American frontier and the colorful cast of characters who inhabited the West.

The following excerpt, from They Called Him Wild Bill, *describes the fateful day in the summer of 1876 when Wild Bill made Deadwood his permanent home. Of this Deadwood day, there are as many stories as stars in a night sky. Dozens of wannabes later claimed to be there when Wild Bill settled in for his long dirt nap. Many attempted to cash in on their fleeting brush with fame by selling phony paraphernalia purported to be Hickok's, while others simply sought stature by saying they had been there.*

So thorough is Rosa's approach that his footnotes even explore the possible poker hands Wild Bill could have been playing when the lights went out: "The actual cards are disputed. Some have it that the fifth card was the Queen of Diamonds. A poker expert commented: If Bill . . . had two pair before the draw. He was well on his way to a full house (3 of a kind plus a pair), which is the fourth highest hand one can get in poker. Mathematically, a full house appears once in 694 hands, so the odds (against getting one) are 693–1. If he had 2 pair after the draw . . . he held the third lowest possible hand, which shows once every 21 hands" (Frank L. Forster to the author, May 15, 1971).

Through simple prose and an engaging storyline, Rosa settles the scene, dismisses the speculation, and walks readers down the long-ago trail that led to the untimely death of the Prince of Pistoleers—James Butler Hickok.

Wild Bill's Presentiment

A week before Wild Bill's death he was heard to remark to a friend, "I feel that my days are numbered; my sun is sinking fast; I know I shall be killed here, something tells me I shall never leave these hills alive; somebody is going to kill me. But I don't know who it is or why he is going to do it. I have killed many men in my day, but I never killed a man yet but what it was kill or get killed with me. But I have two trusty friends, one is my six-shooter and the other is California Joe."

Considering that Charley Utter was his "pardner," it is odd that Hickok should mention California Joe—unless Joe was the "friend" he spoke to. The publication of the story so soon after the assassination indicates that there was some truth in Hickok's alleged belief in his impending death.

On August 1, Wild Bill sat down and wrote to his wife, setting out his feelings for her and hinting at his premonition—indicating pretty clearly that he knew that he was going to die:

DEAD WOOD BLACK HILLS DACOTA August 1st 1876
AGNES DARLING, if such should be we never meet again, while firing my last shot, I will gently breathe the name of my wife— Agnes—and with wishes even for my enemies I will make the plunge and try to swim to the other shore.

J B Hickok Wild Bill

Later in the day Hickok went into the No. 10 saloon, where he was greeted by the bartender, Harry Sam Young. Young claimed in later years that he had first met Hickok in Hays back in 1869 and thanks to Wild Bill had secured employment with the government at Fort Hays. When Wild Bill arrived in Deadwood, one of the first places he went in was Carl Mann's No. 10 saloon, and Young had been the first person he saw. Hickok quickly renewed their old acquaintance and gave his word to Mann that Young was a good boy and could be trusted.

On August 1, Hickok sat in on several games until the early evening. Each time he reserved the right to have his back against the wall—and no one ever refused him. In fact, it is part of the Hickok legend that he always insisted on this precaution, and at this date nothing has been produced to disprove or completely authenticate the story. However, it is in keeping with the actions Wild Bill adopted in public to defend himself against possible attack.

Later in the evening Captain William R. Massie, a former Missouri River pilot who had seen service on the Mississippi, walked in and joined the game. One of the players dropped out, and one of the bystanders took his place. It was Jack McCall. At the end of the evening McCall was broke, and Hickok took pity on him and gave him money enough for his supper. Then, bidding the company good night, Wild Bill made his way back to camp, and was soon inside his blankets.

It has been claimed that earlier in the evening Hickok had stood leaning on the doorjamb of saloon No. 10 watching the crowds bustling past, and had reflected again on his fear and premonition of death. Tom Dosier, one of his acquaintances, had tried to dissuade him from such thoughts, but Wild Bill shook his head and wandered away. Some have even hinted that Wild Bill

The Prince of Pistoleers, James Butler Hickok. (Photo courtesy of Deadwood Historic Preservation Commission, Hickok Collection)

possessed spiritualistic powers, because he often sensed danger and was able to beat his enemies. It is far more likely that years of experience on the plains, among men who held life cheaply, had taught him to be a good judge of men and characteristics—provided they were facing him at the time.

On August 2, Charley Utter was busy arranging final details of a race between his own express and one run by a man named Clippinger. One hundred copies of the *Daily Leader* were being dispatched by coach from Cheyenne to Fort Laramie, and then fifty copies each would be assigned to the rival companies to race the two hundred miles to Deadwood in three days. So Charley was otherwise occupied when Wild Bill went down to saloon No. 10.

Noon came and went and Hickok dressed in his favorite outfit— a Prince Albert frock coat with all the trimmings—meandered into Nuttall and Mann's No. 10 shortly after noon. A nod to Harry Young, and he walked over to where Carl Mann, Charles Rich (the man who had caused all the trouble in the Gold Room in Cheyenne), and Captain Massie were already engaged in a game. There were then about eight people in the room.

At his approach, Mann hailed him and told him to sit down. Hickok hesitated and asked Rich, who had the wall seat, to change round. But he only laughed and told him not to worry—no one was going to attack him. Grudgingly Wild Bill sat down but a few minutes later again asked Rich to change seats. This time all the players good-naturedly ribbed him, and growling uneasily, Wild Bill sat down again. From where he sat, with Rich on his right, Mann on his left, and Massie right in front of him, Hickok had a clear view of the front door, but was conscious of the small door in his rear.

Having beaten Massie the previous evening, Wild Bill was now losing heavily to him. He looked over at Harry Young and asked for fifteen dollars' worth of pocket checks. Young left the bar and came over with them, placed them beside him, then returned to the bar. Shortly before this, the front door swung open and a small, furtive man came in. Some say he was drunk, but others recalled that he gave no such impression as he came up to the bar. Jack McCall stared around. Facing toward him was Wild Bill, but he was busily examining his cards. Quickly he moved down the bar in case Wild Bill looked up—not that Hickok was likely to find much significance in his presence. Reaching the end of the bar, McCall stopped. He was only a few paces behind Hickok's stool.

Wild Bill's attention was on Massie. There was a friendly dispute between them, and Hickok was heard to remark: "The old duffer—he broke me on the hand."

Colorado Charlie Utter, right, and purportedly his brother, Steve, pose at
Wild Bill Hickok's grave shortly after Charlie installed a fitting wooden
headstone at his best friend's final resting place. The grave marker soon
disappeared, whittled away by tourists. Today, an impressive bronze bust
marks the gravesite. (Photo courtesy of Adams Museum, Deadwood, SD)

Those were the last words he spoke. There was a loud bang, and
a shout from McCall: "Damn you, take that!" A smoking pistol was
clutched in his right hand. The time was about 3:00 p.m.

As McCall fired, Wild Bill's head jerked forward, and for some
moments his body remained motionless. Then it toppled back from
the stool to the floor. From his nerveless fingers spilled his cards: the

Ace of Spades, the Ace of Clubs, two black eights, Clubs and Spades, and the Jack of Diamonds. Ever afterward they would be known as "Aces and Eights—The Dead Man's Hand."

For some seconds no one fully realized what had happened. As the report of the shot died away, Captain Massie looked up, puzzled at the noise and the sudden numbness in his left wrist— unaware that Wild Bill was dead. Then he saw McCall, gun in hand, menacing the crowd, and as Hickok's body fell back, he realized what had happened.

Backing toward the rear door, McCall abused the crowd. "Come on ye sons of bitches," he snarled. But all except Carl Mann, on whom the pistol was leveled, ran out the front door. Snapping his pistol at George Shingle and Harry Young (both times it failed to fire), McCall ran out of the back door and mounted the first horse he saw. Unfortunately for him, the owner had slackened the saddle cinch because of the heat, and immediately the saddle turned over, sending McCall sprawling. Gasping for breath, he staggered to his feet and ran down the street, pursued by the excited cry: "Wild Bill is shot! Wild Bill is dead!" At a butcher's shop (said to have been Jacob Shroudy's) he hurried in and tried to hide, but someone used the muzzle end of a Sharps rifle to persuade him to come out, and he gave himself up without a struggle.

Back at the No. 10 some semblance of order was being restored. The doors were locked, and only friends of the deceased and people in authority were allowed in. A brief examination conducted by a hastily organized coroner's court, with C. H. Sheldon as foreman, established that the bullet had entered "the base of the brain, a little to the right of center, passing through in a straight line, making its exit through the right cheek between the upper and lower jaw bones, loosening several of the molar teeth in its passage, and carrying a portion of the cerebellum through the wound. From the nature of the wound death must necessarily have been instantaneous." Having killed Hickok, the ball then lodged in Massie's left wrist.

Word had now reached Colorado Charley, and he hurried into town, where he was joined by Doc Peirce, a barber. The door to No. 10 was unlocked and they were allowed in. In describing the position of Wild Bill's body, Peirce wrote:

> . . . he was lying on his side, with his knees drawn up just as he slid off his stool. We had no chairs in those days—and his fingers were still crimped from holding his poker hand. Charlie Rich, who sat beside him, said he never saw a muscle move. . . . When Bill was shot through the head he bled out quickly, and when he was laid out he looked like a wax figure. I have seen many dead men on the field of battle and in civil life, but Wild Bill was the prettiest corpse I have ever seen. His long moustache was attractive, even in death, and his long tapering fingers looked like marble.

"Calamity Jane—With Wild Bill Hickok in Deadwood, 1876"
from *Calamity Jane: The Woman and the Legend*
James D. McLaird
2005

In his acknowledgments, acclaimed biographer James D. McLaird notes that he didn't set out to write the life story of Martha Jane Canary, merely to determine how she had become famous. When a friend suggested that he begin by separating the fact from the fantasy in the story of Calamity Jane, it set in motion a pursuit that consumed more than a decade of McLaird's life. In his introduction he quotes the editor of the Livingston (Montana) Enterprise, who in 1887 wrote, "A complete and true biography of the life of Calamity Jane would make a large book, more interesting and blood-curdling than all the fictitious stories that have been written of her, but it would never find its way into a Sunday school library." The editor added, at the time of his writing, Calamity Jane "was on a ranch down in Wyoming trying to sober up after a thirty years' drunk."

McLaird notes that in his research, he discovered "the bleak details of Martha's daily life stand in stark contrast to her colorful reputation. Indeed, Martha's career offers an outstanding case study in legend-making." Later the author acknowledges that Calamity, like Buffalo Bill Cody, "is an anomaly in the history of the West. Her importance rests not on the similarity of her life to that of other frontier women, but on the manner in which her life was reshaped to fit a mythic structure glorifying 'the winning of the West.'"

At the conclusion of McLaird's landmark 2005 book, wrought from more than a decade of painstaking research, the author wrote, "Indeed, the adventurous stories attributed to Martha Canary bear *only a remote relationship to actual events in her life. Her career, in fact, may offer the best case study of legend-making in the history of the American West simply because there was so little on which to build: she arrested no outlaws, robbed no banks, and killed no Indians. Instead, hers is the bleak story of poverty, alcoholism, and an unsteady domestic life. She worked as a dance-hall girl, prostitute, waitress, bartender, and cook; she lived with various men she called husbands and expressed affection for her children. Rather than displaying legendary ingredients, her life illustrates a part of western history not often told, the existence of the poor."*

Fifty years after Calamity's death, Doris Day starred in the delightful musical, the flattering Calamity Jane, *in which she sang the Oscar-winning "Secret Love." The resemblance to the actual Calamity could best be described as a screenwriter's fondest fantasy. At various times, the real Calamity was described as a bull-whacker, army scout, prostitute, drunk, nurse, and genuine hell-raiser who could out-drink, out-spit, and out-curse any man. Perhaps she's still howling at the moon.*

Calamity died in 1903 in Deadwood, and was buried next to Wild Bill Hickok in the town's own Boot Hill—Mt. Moriah Cemetery. To this day, tourists flock to visit the graves of Martha Canary and James Butler (Wild Bill) Hickok, who lie buried near each other in Deadwood's Mount Moriah Cemetery. It is commonly supposed that the two had a long-standing relationship that ended in tragedy with Hickok's death on August 2, 1876.

Hickok's biographers, however, discount any serious relationship between the two figures, suggesting he was too fastidious a man to associate with such a dissolute woman. Frank J. Wilstach, whose 1926 biography *Wild Bill Hickok: The Prince of the Pistoleers* did much to secure Hickok's twentieth-century popularity, labeled any relationship with Calamity "gossip" and said that "the report that he [Hickok] was associated with the woman at any time seems to be pure moonshine." Similarly, Joseph Rosa, the foremost modern Hickok scholar, concludes that "of all the women associated in any

A one-woman cyclone, Calamity Jane assumes a studio pose.
Though her life seldom resembled the tall tales that made
her famous, biographer James D. McLaird says the sometime-
prostitute and confirmed gambler was "thoroughly masculine."
Wild Bill Hickok once gave her $20 on the condition she take a
bath. (Photo courtesy of the Adams Museum, Deadwood, S.D.)

way with Wild Bill, she [Martha] had the least to do with him, yet she is always spoken of in the same breath when Hickok's women friends are mentioned."

Stories connecting Martha Canary and James Butler Hickok began appearing even during Martha's lifetime. For example, an Omaha newspaper in 1892 referred to her as "an old side part-ner of Wild Bill, the notorious desperado who was assassinated in Deadwood. Jane was in Deadwood at the time and was among the first to place a pillow under the head of the dying man and min-ister to his wants." Deadwood newspapers at the time of Martha's death on August 1, 1903, also linked her to Hickok, but showed con-siderable confusion. First it was suggested that Martha asked to be buried next to her old friend, and then, only a few days later, it was stated that he was her "former husband" and that they lived "as man and wife in a cabin along Deadwood gulch." In the ensuing years, accounts became increasingly fanciful, with some writers even changing Martha's death date to coincide with Hickok's. For example, Harry (Sam) Young asserted that she died August 2, 1906, "the same day and month, and the same hour, Wild Bill was assassinated thirty years before."

The truth concerning the relationship between Martha and Wild Bill may never be determined. Clearly, neither fantasizing romanti-cists nor hostile detractors are completely correct. Martha was far more attractive a personality than critics suggest, but less intimate with Hickok than romanticists imagine. Martha's *Life and Adventures* asserts in a matter-of-fact manner that she first met Hickok at Fort Laramie in June 1876 and traveled to Deadwood in his company. She refers to him in her book only as a friend.

Upon her return to Fort Fetterman about June 27 after visit-ing Crook's army, Martha evidently meandered to Fort Laramie and the nearby road ranches. A traveler to the Black Hills, Charles Grant, recalled meeting her at Hat Creek Station, about sixty miles from Fort Laramie. They first became acquainted when "she asked me if I had any chewing tobacco," said Grant. "Fortunately for her I had some, and gave her half a plug." During that meeting, which he recalled lasted only a half-hour, she explained that she had attempted to join a military expedition (Grant thought Custer's), but "the soldiers had refused to permit her to accompany the command." After talking with Grant, Martha probably wandered to Fort Laramie. Coincidently, Wild Bill Hickok, who with his friend Charles (Colorado Charlie) Utter had organized a wagon train of gold seekers to go to the Black Hills, also visited the post.

Hickok already was a well-known frontiersman. Born in Troy Grove, Illinois, on May 27, 1837, he first journeyed west with his brother, Lorenzo, in 1856. He became a spy and wagoneer for the Union during the Civil War. But it was a controversial shooting incident at Rock Creek stage station in Nebraska in 1861 that propelled him to fame. Details of the Rock Creek event are disputed, but Hickok and others at the station killed several members of the McCanles family. An exaggerated version of that incident, combined with other heroic adventures, appeared in the February 1867 *Harper's Monthly,* bringing Hickok national prominence. The author of the Story, George Ward Nichols, portrayed the McCanles family as a gang of proslavery villains and claimed that Hickok single-handedly fought off his opponents with gun and knife. A few months after the appearance of Nichols's article, Hickok was featured in a dime novel, *Wild Bill, The Indian Slayer* (July 1867), helping enlarge his reputation. Later, in Hays City and Abilene, Kansas, he acted as deputy U.S. marshal, army scout, and law officer, service which also enhanced his stature.

Although many admired Hickok, others despised him for his showy dress, his itchy trigger-finger, and his compulsive gambling. Legends say he killed thirty-six men, or perhaps a hundred, but his most careful biographer, Joseph Rosa, concludes the killings numbered about ten.

Hickok spent much of his time in 1874 and 1875 in Cheyenne, Wyoming. There, on March 5, 1876, Hickok married Agnes Lake Thatcher after a long acquaintance that began in 1871 in Abilene.

W. F. Warren, the Methodist minister in Cheyenne who married the couple, wrote in the remarks column of the church register, "I don't think they meant it," but he may have been mistaken. After a two-week visit to her family in Cincinnati, Ohio, Hickok returned alone to Cheyenne. He then joined the gold rush to the Black Hills, evidently intending to send for Agnes as soon as he was established.

Planning to lead a wagon train of gold seekers into the Black Hills, Hickok traveled to and from St. Louis and Cheyenne several times during the spring of 1876, recruiting and organizing the proposed expedition. The Cheyenne newspaper reported on April 14 that "Wild Bill still lingers with us," spending his time "stuffing newcomers and tenderfeet of all descriptions with tales of his prowess and his wonderful discoveries of diamond caves, etc., which he describes as being located 'up north.'" At some point he met Colorado Charley Utter, who intended to establish a Black Hills transportation line, and the two seem to have merged their efforts. The Hickok-Utter party evidently left Cheyenne on June 27 for the Black Hills, reaching John Hunton's road ranch on June 30. Hunton dutifully noted in his diary, "Large party of B. Hillers passed with 'Wild Bill.'"

Hickok and his companions tarried briefly fifteen miles north of Fort Laramie at Government Farm, a popular stopping point for wagon trains. There they hoped to join other parties for security against Indians. The party also took on an unexpected new member, Martha Canary. Joseph (White Eye) Anderson, one of Hickok's associates, remembered that when they arrived at Fort Laramie, an officer requested they take Martha with them. It being "just after payday," she "had been on a big drunk with the soldiers and had been having a hell of a time of it." She was now residing in the guard house, "very drunk and near naked." Steve Utter, Charley's brother, agreed to take her along. Anderson added: "The officer furnished a suit of soldiers' underclothes, and the rest of us furnished her with sufficient clothes to wear, including a buckskin costume and a broad-brimmed hat. White Eye thought her reasonably attractive when she was sober, cleaned up, and dressed."

Many years later, White Eye Anderson wrote that this "was the first time that Wild Bill had met her and he surely did not have any use for her." White Eye claimed that Martha's companion during the trip to the Hills was Steve Utter. Likewise, John Hunton, who had become acquainted with Hickok in 1874-75, was convinced that Wild Bill had not met Martha before this journey by wagon train in 1876.

Martha was not the only camp follower with Hickok's party. Although many of the people in the wagon train were prospectors, gamblers, and saloon men, recalled Anderson, there also were as many as fourteen "ladies of easy virtue." John Gray, a member of the party who later became a prominent mining figure in the Hills, recalled that the party included Calamity Jane, Madame Moustache, and Dirty Em, "each of whom will be remembered by old-timers."

The trip from Fort Laramie to the Black Hills took about two weeks, during which Anderson and Martha became well acquainted. He estimated her age to be twenty-five (she was twenty). According to Anderson, Martha could drive a team of mules as well as any man. Her bullwhacking skills proved valuable to the party, he said. She would get them over the rough places "with a black snake whip and lots of cussing." Martha also was good with a rifle and six-shooter. One day when a coyote was spotted in the distance, the men fired at it with their rifles and missed, but Martha, said Anderson, killed it "with a six-shooter when it was over one hundred yards away." Besides these "masculine" activities, Martha helped Anderson, the party's cook, prepare the food, which led him to conclude she was a "big-hearted woman." However, he also recalled that when the party gathered near the campfire each night, she "told some of the toughest stories I ever heard and there would always be a big crowd come over to the campfire to hear her talk."

According to Anderson, Hickok avoided Martha's campfire stories, but he nevertheless frequently came into contact with her during the trip. This was because Hickok had a keg of whiskey and invited his friends to help themselves. Martha "hit it more often than anyone else," recalled Anderson. But each time she wanted a drink, she had

LAMITY JANE "AT
LD BILL'S "GRAVE
JULY 1903

PARKER ART SHOP
DEADWOOD, S.D.

Just a month before her own death in August 1903, Calamity Jane strikes a pose at Wild Bill Hickok's gravesite in Deadwood's Mt. Moriah Cemetery. She would join Wild Bill as one of Deadwood's most famous permanent residents. (Photo courtesy of Adams Museum, Deadwood, SD)

to request the tin cup from Hickok. "She would say, 'Mr. Hickok, I'm dry again.' Once he told her to go slow, that others were dry too."

These anecdotes obscure the difficulty of wagon travel to the Black Hills. Only a few weeks after the Hickok party made the trip, a party of eight men including journalist Leander P. Richardson, left Fort Laramie. From the beginning, "sand-gnats" harrassed them. These pesky insects, Richardson wrote, "darted into our eyes, crawled into our nostrils, buzzed in our ears, and wriggled down our necks in a most annoying fashion." In addition, they had to cross "deep and precipitous gulches," and after a cold, drizzling rain, all of their party caught colds. The rainfall also produced mud that clung so tight to the wheels that it became necessary every hundred yards "to dismount and pry it away with a crow-bar." It is likely the Hickok party's journey was similarly demanding.

Upon reaching the southern Black Hills, the Hickok party stopped briefly in Custer City. Most of the town's residents had left after learning of the gold discoveries in Deadwood. Those remaining recalled that Hickok stayed in a little house on the banks of French Creek. After the visit of "Wild Bill and his crew of depraved women" in 1876, a reporter noted, Hickok was considered by the people of Custer "as a 'bum' and hard citizen who sought only the lower strata of society for associates."

However, Hickok soon left Custer, arriving in Deadwood about July 12 with several companions. Newspaperman Richard B. Hughes described their spectacular parade down Deadwood's main street. Accompanying Hickok were "four other characters—also of considerable notoriety," Charley and Steve Utter, "Bloody Dick" Seymour, and Calamity Jane, "who basked chiefly in the reflected glory of their leader." Their entry was designed to attract attention, Hughes added, as they "rode the entire length of Main Street, mounted on good horses and clad in complete suits of buckskin, every suit which carried sufficient fringe to make a considerable buckskin rope." Black Hills pioneer John S. McClintock, who learned of the party's arrival the next day, remembered two women in Hickok's party, Calamity Jane and Kitty Arnold. After arriving, they pitched their tents along Whitewood Creek, according to White Eye Anderson. Martha did not remain with them, however. "Wild Bill, the Utter boys, Pie, my brother Charlie, and myself camped there," said White Eye, "and sometimes Calamity Jane came to camp when she got hungry."

Confirming Martha's presence in Deadwood, the *Black Hills Pioneer* of July 15 reported, "'Calamity Jane' has arrived." Martha was the only member of the Hickok party whose arrival was announced, perhaps because she was well known from her earlier trips to the

Hills. She immediately became a dance-hall celebrity. Those who assume she was too dissolute and masculine to be attractive missed essential qualities of her character. Even detractor Captain Jack Crawford, who believed Hickok's "name should in no way be associated with Calamity Jane's," admitted that she was "a good-hearted woman and under different environments would have made a good wife and mother." But growing up in mining camps without parental supervision resulted in her living "in a wild, unnatural manner."

In her *Life and Adventures,* Martha omitted her dance-hall career, instead claiming that during June she served "as a pony express rider carrying the U.S. mail between Deadwood and Custer, a distance of fifty miles, over one of the roughest trails in the Black Hills country." Although previous riders were "robbed of their packages, mail and money," Martha said she was not bothered by road agents because of her "reputation as a rider and quick shot." Her story is fanciful. Charley Utter did establish an express mail service in July, perhaps the "pony express" Martha mentions, but no source indicates she rode for it or any other mail service. In fact, her autobiography is somewhat contradictory. It states that she "remained around Deadwood all that summer visiting all the camps within an area of one hundred miles," which, if true, left little time to carry the mail.

White Eye Anderson recalled the period differently. Shortly after their arrival in Deadwood, he remembered, Martha asked the members of the Hickok party for a loan. "I can't do business in these old buckskins," she explained. "I ain't got the show the other girls have." The men all contributed, said Anderson, but Hickok's $20 came with a request that she "wash behind her ears." Martha agreed and took a bath in the creek, even asking Steve Utter to "wash her body thoroughly with perfumed soap." Then she purchased "a good outfit of female clothes." When Martha returned to the Hickok camp a few days later, said Anderson, she "pulled up her dress, rolled down her stocking and took out a roll of greenbacks" and repaid the money she had borrowed. She said business had been good, but she "didn't express it in just that way."

Anderson also remembered that Hickok refused repayment, saying, "At least she looks like a woman now."

John S. McClintock similarly recalled that Martha figured "conspicuously in the many dance halls." In these popular dance halls, or hurdy-gurdy houses, young women were made available as dancing partners. Usually there was no charge for dancing, but at the end of each dance, men took their partners to the bar to purchase drinks, with the proprietor sharing profits from the sales with the dance-hall girls. The Deadwood newspaper described the hurdy-gurdy dances in considerable detail:

> To witness a dance at one of our hurdy gurdy houses, we think
> would be interesting to some of our eastern friends unaccus-
> tomed to such scenes, particularly after the dance has been
> under way for several hours, and the participants in the dance
> have had sufficient time to become well filled up with the choice
> brands of whisky usually sold at such places. The whisky soon
> limbers them up and the motley crowd vie with each other in
> showing their own peculiar fancy steps, while their partners, the
> frail sisters of the town, put on their sweetest smiles and enter
> into the amusement with vigor.

A prospector, George Stokes, said that when he saw Martha she was wearing "a ten-dollar Stetson with a cowman's purple handkerchief around her neck" and "danced with everybody and promenaded to the bar, as was the custom, after every dance."

Generally, these dancing establishments remained opened most of the night and although the girls were not necessarily prostitutes, it was not uncommon for them to engage in the oldest profession. Some accounts identify E. A. Swearingen's "Gem" as the establishment where Martha initially danced in Deadwood. Swearingen had entered Deadwood with a bull team in May 1876. "He arrived on Monday and by the next Saturday he had a dance hall running," recalled the Deadwood newspaper, noting that the flimsy structure was built of lumber and canvas. That summer, he had only three women available for dancing: Mrs. Swearingen, Kitty Arnold, and Calamity Jane. Needing another dancer, a young man "was dressed in feminine garb, corseted and padded, with closely shingled hair," said the newspaper, and sold liquor as easily as the women.

Swearingen's dance hall had a bad reputation. McClintock said "it would require an abler pen than mine to portray anything approaching a true picture of the inside workings of that notorious den of iniquity." Swearingen made regular trips to other towns to recruit new women, enticing them to the Hills with promises of jobs in hotels or with families. If, after reaching Deadwood, the young women refused to work in his dance hall, they had to fend for themselves. Despite the Gem's unsavory reputation, said McClintock, Swearingen drew support from Deadwood's "so-called leading citizen" as well as from "residents and floaters of the underworld." His dance hall became Deadwood's "chief attraction."

Deadwood bartender Sam Young, who first met Martha during the 1875 Black Hills expedition, recalled not only that Martha worked at the Gem but said she helped Swearingen recruit other young women as well. Young became reacquainted with Martha while he was playing a game of faro in Jim Pencil's saloon. Since she was broke, Young gave her "a five-dollar greenback," which she spent immediately on drinks, "and in a short time she was in a wild state of intoxication." Young claimed that Swearingen once asked Martha to go to Sidney, Nebraska, "to white slave for him." She returned with ten girls, having "captivated them with exaggerated stories of the immense wealth in Black Hills and the large amount of money to be made." Young also recalled Martha's "habits were thoroughly masculine," and that she frequently danced with girls just as the men did.

William B. Lull, a Methodist minister's son who arrived in the Black Hills in 1875 in search of gold, likewise recalled Martha working in the dance halls. Lull, nicknamed "New York Billie," became the manager of Porter's Hotel, which catered to dance-hall girls and gamblers. Martha was one of the hotel's occupants. She also served

refreshments at the Bella Union, remembered Lull, who characterized her as a "lone Wolf" and "born gambler" addicted to the game of
faro. During the time she stayed at the hotel, Martha became seriously ill with mountain fever or typhoid. Against her will, Lull sent
for a doctor and organized the other hotel girls to take turns caring
for her. Although Martha had to be forced to take her medicine, she
afterwards thanked Lull and gave him a tintype of her.

According to Leander Richardson, for a while Martha main-
tained her own sporting establishment in competition with Kitty
Austin (Arnold). Richardson remembered that Martha had arrived in
Deadwood with only "a suit of men's clothing and a progressive jag,"
so dress was a problem for her. Although Kitty "was the prettiest"
and had a lavish wardrobe, Martha "could outride, outdrink, and out-
shoot" her, and occasionally, after consuming sufficient liquor, would
ride "up and down the street howling like an Indian" and "shoot in all
the windows of Miss Austin's vaunted temple of Terpsichore."

White Eye Anderson related one memorable dance-hall episode
involving Martha and "Tid Bit," a redhead from Salt Lake City who,
like Martha, entered the Hills with the Hickok party. Tid Bit "agreed
to entertain" a fellow nicknamed Laughing Sam. But the gold dust
he gave her as payment turned out to be "brass filings and black
sand." Learning of the deception, Martha borrowed Charley Utter's
"two big, ivory handled six-shooters," and walked to the saloon where
Laughing Sam and Bummer Dan ran a faro game. Anderson and his
friends followed "to see the fun." Martha, with guns in hand, informed
the crowd what Laughing Sam had done. "I never heard a man get
such a cussing as she gave him," Anderson said, adding that Martha
forced Laughing Sam to give Tid Bit "two twenty dollar gold pieces."

Another popular story identifies Martha as the culprit who dis-
rupted a theatrical presentation. According to Leander Richardson,
Jack Langrishe was performing *The Streets of New York* that summer. One scene in that play depicts two female characters deciding
to commit suicide and the hero bursting into the room to save them.
At this intense moment in the drama, a woman "clad in yellow silk

trimmed with bright green" loudly "cleared her mouth of its cargo of tobacco juice, and cried in disdainful tones that were perfectly audible all over the house: 'Oh, H——L! That's a put up job.'" After a "momentary lull," there was a "howl of laughter, in which even the dying actresses were forced to join." However, Martha may not have been the person guilty of the expectoration and exclamation. In a later article, Richardson identified Martha's rival, Kitty Arnold, as the tobacco-spitting woman.

Encounters between Martha and the first minister in the Black Hills, the Reverend Henry Weston Smith, also became the gist for legend. Sam Young recalled that during the minister's first sermon in Deadwood, five dance-hall girls attended, and Martha, in "an intoxicated condition, snatched his old hat from his hand," announcing to the listeners, "You sinners, dig down in your pokes, now; this old fellow looks as though he were broke and I want to collect about two hundred dollars for him." According to White Eye Anderson, at another service the minister talked about money being the root of all evil. Martha told him "that she didn't care very much for the money, just as long as she had plenty of the root she was satisfied."

"WILD BILL HICKOK AND HIS MAGIC TOUCH" AND "THAT'S NO MAN— THAT'S CALAMITY JANE" FROM *TALES OF THE BLACK HILLS* HELEN REZATTO

1983

As a youngster growing up in North Dakota, Helen Rezatto would vacation in South Dakota's emerald oasis and listen to the legends and lore of the last region of America to be mapped. She reveled in stories of Wild West gunfighters, gold-seekers, fierce Indian warriors, and men who carved mountains. And, she remembered.

Later, when Rezatto made her permanent home in the Black Hills, she captured a collection of historical vignettes that spanned a century, from Custer's Expedition of 1874 and the legends of Bear Butte to colorful Chinese funerals and a memorial-in-the-making known as Crazy Horse. She also examined many of the memorable characters who once walked the streets of Deadwood, including Preacher Smith, Doc Peirce, Lame Johnny, Jack Langrishe, Dr. Valentine McGillycuddy, and a gallery of Deadwood Dicks.

In the following excerpt taken from Rezatto's 1983 book, Tales of the Black Hills, we explore two of the Western legends who helped brand Deadwood for time immemorial—Wild Bill Hickok and Calamity Jane. In her "informal history," the author distinguishes between fact and fable, yet captures much of the mystique in these favored lives who continue to generate motion pictures, scholarly biographies, and tall tales more than a century after their physical departure from this earth.

Wild Bill Hickok and His Magic Touch

Wild Bill Hickok, as everyone knows, was the fastest gun in the Wild West. He was also an accomplished magician. He lived in a tent in Deadwood, Dakota Territory, for only about six weeks while prospecting gold during the Black Hills Gold Rush in 1876. An inveterate gambler, this famous Kansas marshal, carelessly sitting with his back to the door, was shot in the back while playing poker in the Saloon No. 10 in Deadwood.

And that's it—that's the extent of his accomplishments in the entire Black Hills. He didn't even shoot anyone. Yet, Wild Bill is hailed as the most illustrious person ever to be a Black Hills resident, however briefly. There must be magic somewhere to explain how his personality dominated Black Hills history and legend, which are hopelessly entangled and can never be clearly separated, especially about Wild Bill Hickok.

Maybe he had a magic wand, a secret weapon that still transmits powerful signals. Or sleight-of-hand tricks that have mesmerized the entire populace for over a century. Something like that.

Wild Bill Hickok was saluted as the Prince of Pistoleers. His friend and one-time employer, Buffalo Bill Cody, said: "He was the most deadly shot with rifle and pistols that ever lived." A great many other eye-witnesses to his shooting prowess said the same thing. Wild Bill was the gunman par excellence with an estimated 100 shootings to his credit or discredit, not counting Civil War rebels and Indians.

Wild Bill was born James Butler Hickok in Troy Grove, Illinois, in 1837, and early in life demonstrated great talent in using guns. When he became a youthful stagecoach driver in Nebraska, he got into a fight with the McCanles horse-stealing gang and single-handedly, with lightning-like rapidity, shot and killed nine of them. Some say three victims were innocent bystanders. The lenient frontier jury acquitted him on self-defense. From that time on, everyone on the frontier began calling him "Wild Bill" very admiringly.

During the Civil War, Wild Bill acquitted himself well as scout and sharpshooter for the Union Army. After the war, to earn a living, he tried homesteading, bullwhacking, stagecoach driving, scouting, and gambling, his obsessive occupation.

In 1867, Hickok scouted for General George Custer in Kansas, and the two controversial long-hairs became good friends. In Custer's only book, *My Life on the Plains,* he wrote: "Wild Bill was a strange character, just the one which a novelist might gloat over. . . . He was one of the most perfect types of physical manhood I ever saw, the most famous scout on the Plains." Custer was convinced that Wild Bill never killed a man except in self-defense and concluded "that his skill in the use of rifle and pistol was unerring."

Various biographers relate many thrilling episodes in which Hickok killed countless Indians and outlaws and had many narrow escapes, including a fight with a grizzly bear. But he led a charmed life—for awhile.

Everyone who ever knew him or wrote about him agrees that his shooting prowess was spectacular. He could hit a dime tossed into the air nine out of ten times; he could drill bullets into the cork of a bottle without hitting the glass, and all at twenty-five paces or more. Although he had to cock the hammer each time he shot and never appeared to aim, he could handle two guns, firing simultaneously from the hips and never miss, whether in target practice or in life-or-death situations.

Wild Bill and his fast guns were just what some of the lawless frontier towns wanted—a peace officer. He was appointed deputy United States marshal to clean up the rip-roaring towns of Hays City and Abilene, both in Kansas. And he did, acting as judge, jury, and executioner for suspicious characters and thus fulfilling his murderous duties as peace officer. He left innumerable corpses strewn throughout Kansas, all presumably killed in self-defense.

Women were always attracted to charismatic Wild Bill and his handsome, clean appearance and charming manners. He had a number of romances but Calamity Jane wasn't one of them. Then he became enamored of a daring circus acrobat and equestrienne, Agnes Lake Thatcher. Widow Thatcher was eleven years older than he; and,

Wild Bill Hickok found his final resting place in Deadwood's Mount Moriah Cemetery. An impressive bronze bust of the famed gunfighter marks his grave in a cemetery that has recently witnessed a comprehensive, three-year, $3.4 million restoration. Martha "Calamity Jane" Canary is buried in a neighboring grave. (Photo by Nyla Griffith)

according to her photograph, was not pretty. Nevertheless, Wild Bill married her in March 1876, in Cincinnati, Ohio. He gallantly gave his age as 45 instead of 39 so he would be older than the false age his bride assigned to herself.

After a two-week honeymoon, Agnes went to stay with her daughter in Cincinnati. Wild Bill left on the train for Cheyenne, WY, to make plans for joining the Black Hills Gold Rush.

On a memorable day in June, 1876, Wild Bill Hickok and Calamity Jane, all duded up in fringed buckskins and white stetsons, galloped into Deadwood Gulch as outriders for the long, Colorado Charlie Utter wagon train from Cheyenne which delivered the first whores to Deadwood. The cumbersome ox-train blocked the traffic in the gold camp, jammed with an estimated 10,000 to 25,000 prospectors, reputed to be the entire floating population of the west.

Wild Bill and the Utter brothers set up headquarters in a tent in the crowded, twisting gulch packed with gold-crazed prospectors and a jumble of wagons with oxen, horses, and mules trampling manure into the muddy, stinking main street. The sounds of pounding hammers and screechy music mingled with the cries of hawkers selling soap and peanuts and knives. Gamblers and hustlers exhorted the men to try their luck at faro, poker, and other games of chance. Adding to the bedlam were the oaths of bull-whackers, the cracks of their long black whips, the bawling of cattle, and the braying of mules. These were the sounds of Deadwood when Wild Bill Hickok arrived in the rambunctious gold camp.

In lawless Deadwood, Wild Bill kept a low profile, not capitalizing on his already widespread reputation as a gunfighter, scout, and lawman. He prospected a little, wrote loving letters to his wife Agnes, did some target practice. But he spent most of his time gambling, his greatest obsession.

On August 2nd, a significant date in Black Hills history, Wild Bill was playing poker with his friends in the Saloon No. 10. Inexplicably, the Kansas marshal with many enemies, sat with his back to the door. In burst Crooked Nose Jack McCall, a common gunslinger, and shot Wild Bill in the back of the head. Wild Bill Hickok died instantly. He was holding black aces and eights, known forever after as the "Deadman's Hand."

Several Hickok promoters claimed for years that Wild Bill had both guns out and cocked before he fell over the poker table. Others say he never had time to reach. So go the contradictions of the legend.

Jack McCall ran out of the saloon with his gun smoking, and outraged citizens chased the assassin yelling "Wild Bill's been shot! Wild Bill is dead!"

The assassin was eventually captured in a much-disputed location on Deadwood's main street—without Calamity Jane's help, as she later insisted.

Jack McCall was tried the next day in the Bella Union theater before a packed house, eager for entertainment. Because Deadwood was legally Indian territory, the judge and jury had no jurisdiction; they just went through the motions of the fake trial. Jack McCall testified that he had shot Wild Bill to avenge the death of his brother by Wild Bill's gun in Kansas.

Judge W. Y. Kuykendall accepted the revenge motive and acquitted McCall in a farcical trial typical of frontier justice. McCall did not leave town until he was good and ready. Eventually, he was arrested in Wyoming, United States territory, where he bragged about killing Wild Bill Hickok He was arrested and brought to Yankton, the capital of Dakota Territory. In this second trial, Jack McCall was convicted in a federal court, and on March 1, 1877, was hanged for the murder of Wild Bill Hickok and buried with the rope around his neck.

After Hickok's murder, Colorado Charlie Utter and his brother Steve carried Wild Bill's body to their tent where Doc Peirce, a loquacious barber acted as undertaker "on the prettiest corpse I've ever seen." Everyone in the gulch, including a wailing Calamity Jane, traipsed through the tent to see if the fastest gun in the west was really dead.

The Utter brothers buried Wild Bill in the Ingleside area of Deadwood, the first boot hill, and placed a wooden marker above the grave with this inscription:

Wild Bill
J. B. Hickok
Killed by the assassin Jack McCall
Deadwood, Black Hills
August 2, 1876
Pard we will meet again in the
Happy Hunting Grounds to part no more
Good bye
Colorado Charlie, C. H. Utter

Three years later, in 1879, the Utter brothers returned to Deadwood and with John McClintock and another Deadwood man, dug up Wild Bill's coffin and struggled up the steep hill carrying the wooden coffin to Mount Moriah, the new cemetery.

McClintock, who many years later wrote *Pioneer Days in the Black Hills,* described opening the casket and finding that both Wild Bill's carbine and his corpse were in a perfect state of preservation. His clothes were decomposed and the body was exposed to the hips and coated with lime. McClintock poked the corpse with a stick in many places but did not discover any soft spots.

This well-publicized story gave rise to the rumor that Wild Bill's body was petrified and impervious to ordinary decomposition presumably because of the god-like status of the deceased. Or Doc Peirce must have been a better undertaker than anyone thought.

Through the years several gravemarkers and statues were destroyed by vandals in Mount Moriah cemetery, including two large monuments, one a bust and the other a life-size statue of Wild Bill.

Wild Bill's friends and enemies, including the first Black Hills tourists, began to make pilgrimages to the grave. Hickok's widow Agnes came; as did Buffalo Bill Cody and Captain Jack Crawford, the poet-scout, who wrote several poems about Wild Bill while sitting on his grave. And of course Calamity Jane came often, even having her picture taken at the grave site.

Like his friend Custer, Wild Bill's death, a violent death, complete with dramatic irony, conferred on Wild Bill Hickok an immortality he could never have earned even if he had lived to be one hundred years old with his shooting skill intact.

Another reason for Wild Bill's increasing notoriety is that in 1885, nine years after his death, author Edward Wheeler (pseudonym Ned Buntline) used his name for a hero of numerous dime novels with a western setting which featured well-known western characters as fictionized heroes and heroines.

Wild Bill was also the subject of countless articles in western pulp magazines whose editors were not concerned about facts and historical accuracy. Eventually serious historians and biographers wrote about Wild Bill Hickok, each presenting his or her version of a much-disputed life. Was he a fair, dedicated peace officer who killed only in self-defense, as Custer insisted? Or was he an instinctive killer who gloried in using his magic gun at the slightest provocation? Who knows?

Almost every author who wrote a newspaper or magazine feat about Deadwood or a history of the Black Hills openly admitted to having known Wild Bill personally—or else the writer's grandfather had. The number of people who claimed to have been kibitzing at that celebrated poker game in Saloon No. 10 when the Kansas marshal was murdered would suggest that the log cabin saloon, which later burned, must have been larger than a Roman amphitheater.

In the twentieth century, the motion picture industry discovered both Wild Bill Hickok and Calamity Jane. Many movies dramatized the make-believe romance between them. The movie screen also added new dimensions to Wild Bill's exploits while cleaning up and prettifying Calamity Jane.

Ever since Wild Bill was murdered in 1876, Deadwood residents have been proud that he died there and delighted to claim this six-week-resident as a native son.

A few spoil-sports have pointed out that Wild Bill did nothing for Deadwood except to die there. But that was plenty. He has become the patron saint of commerce throughout the Hills, and especially in Deadwood, where all types of stores and miscellaneous merchandise have been named for Wild Bill Hickok. The commercial exploitation combined with ersatz history provides signs, often contradictory, about the exact location of the original Saloon No. 10 and the exact spot where assassin Jack McCall was captured. The graves of Wild Bill and Calamity Jane high above Deadwood in Mount Moriah cemetery are popular tourist attractions.

Yes, there are many understandable reasons why this sleight-of-hand artist has become one of the most enduring legends in American folklore. Wild Bill personified the ideal hero of the west: he was both a gunfighter and a lawman on horseback, the supreme role of command and influence, endowed with the phallic symbolism of the towering horseman with a pointed gun. He lived by the gun and he died by the gun—and that's frontier justice. Today, he is a dominant figure in western mythology, one to be cherished and remembered, like the Wild West itself.

There is also another reason why Wild Bill Hickok will live forever—he had the magic touch.

That's No Man—That's Calamity Jane

"I was considered the most reckless and daring rider and one of the best shots in the western country. And I was at all times with the men where there was excitement and adventures to be had." So says Calamity Jane in her autobiography written by a ghost writer.

Truer words than these were never spoken by that frontier roustabout and inventive liar known as Calamity Jane. Perhaps this quoted example of her truthfulness is the exception to prove the rule because much of what she publicized about herself was simply gross exaggeration or an outrageous lie—like the sensational fib about her and Wild Bill Hickok being lovers.

Separating fact from fiction about the woman (even some doubt about that) who is undoubtedly "Queen of the Wild West" is mostly

The one-woman cyclone known as Calamity Jane. Though she frequently swore she could out-spit, out-cuss, and out-ride any man, modern-day biographers contend she may have been famous simply for being famous. This photo, circa 1876, was later found under a building. (Photo courtesy of the Adams Museum, Deadwood, SD)

impossible. Calamity Jane has become a legend. And legends are notoriously difficult to pin down to origins, verifiable facts, and clear-cut roles.

Take the contradictions about her appearance; she has been described as both beautiful and ugly, with both red hair and black raven tresses. Authors have described her as (the) "roughest-looking human I ever saw" and "extremely pretty." Undoubtedly, she aged quickly from the degenerate life she led.

At last, historians have decided that Calamity Jane was born Martha Canary around 1850—give or take a year or two—in Princeton, Missouri. When she was a young girl she began frolicking around the frontier in Montana, Utah, Colorado, Kansas, Wyoming, and Dakota Territory (particularly in the Black Hills).

During her lifetime she was at various times a bullwhacker, a scout, a teamster, a prostitute, a howling drunk, a laundress, a cook, a sharp-shooter, a prospector, and a home nurse. "Reckless" and "daring" she certainly was, especially where there were men, excitement and adventure—as she says in her spurious autobiography.

However, this rare little pamphlet which she sold on the streets and in saloons when she was down and out can be mostly discounted as history. It is a tall, tall tale typical of the frontier and an example of Calamity's often boozy imagination.

In her autobiography, which should be labeled "fiction," Calamity explains how she acquired her name. During an Indian ambush, her comrade, a Captain Eagan, was injured in the fight, but dare-devil Calamity galloped up beside him and lifted him onto her own horse. Then she raced for the fort holding the wounded man in front of the saddle. Later, she claimed the grateful captain bestowed her nickname as though he were crowning a queen: "I name you Calamity Jane, the Heroine of the Plains."

Dora DuFran, a notorious brothel madam in the Black Hills, and a close friend of Calamity's later wrote a book about her, *Low Down on Calamity Jane*. Madam DuFran had another explanation of how Calamity acquired her name: "If anyone was sick in camp, it was 'send for Jane!' Where calamity was, there was Jane; and so she was christened Calamity Jane."

Watson Parker, dean of Black Hills historians, suggests that the most likely story about how she got her name was that Calamity Jane's paramours were generally visited by some venereal "calamity."

Even though at various times she worked as a prostitute, especially when she needed money for drinks, Calamity often dressed like a man in buckskins, a big campaign hat hiding her hair, and packing six-shooters which she was an expert at using. How she relished the huge joke of passing herself off as a man, especially when she wanted a job as a bullwhacker or teamster. Like the typical macho image of the western hero, she could drink, cuss, ride horseback, shoot, and chew tobacco. Sometimes she even danced with the "soiled doves" in the hurdy-gurdy houses.

No wonder a common refrain on the frontier when an exhibitionist in pants shot up a saloon, put on a show cracking a bull whip, or won all the turkeys in a shooting match was, "That's no man—that's Calamity Jane!"

Perhaps it is true, as some biographers have suggested, that Calamity's fondness for playing both feminine and masculine roles indicated bi-sexuality.

Dressed like a man, Calamity Jane first entered the Black Hills in 1875 with the Jenney-Newton scientific expedition, whom the government had commissioned to verify the glowing reports of the Custer Expedition of 1874 about gold discoveries in the Black Hills.

She probably got herself hired as a teamster driving a supply wagon and impressed the boss with her working vocabulary of obscenities. Then someone said, "That's no man—that's Calamity Jane!" and sent her back to Fort Laramie. But she sneaked back, and therefore first came into the Black Hills with the Jenney-Newton Expedition.

Thus, Calamity Jane was the third non-Indian woman to penetrate the Black Hills: the first was Sarah Campbell (Aunt Sally), a Negro cook for the Custer Expedition in the summer of 1874; and the second was the revered Annie Tallent, a white woman with the illegal Russell-Collins Party in late 1874. Therefore, Calamity was certainly a Black Hills pioneer of 1875; and depending on whether from a white or from an Indian point of view, she deserves some credit for that distinction.

Calamity was a versatile liar. She lied when she said she scouted for General Custer; she probably never met the ill-fated general. She lied about being a scout for General George Crook in 1875 when he ordered the illegal prospectors out of the Black Hills which belonged exclusively to the Sioux Indians.

At least once, she told the truth about her scouting; she really was a scout for General Crook at Fort Fetterman in May, 1876. The proof is that her name was listed on the records of Frank Grouard, chief of scouts, and she is also mentioned as being there in the diaries of several of the soldiers with Crook.

Undoubtedly, she was an excellent scout. She knew the terrain and the wagon ruts and the saloons at the end of the trails. An expert shot with both rifle and pistol, she was a roughneck with characteristics of both sexes, a dramatic concoction of good and bad; certainly she could cope with the hardships of the wilderness as well as any man.

Calamity Jane made a spectacular entrance into Deadwood Gulch at the height of the gold rush in June, 1876, when she and Wild Bill Hickok were both outriders with the Colorado Charlie Utter wagon train from Cheyenne, Wyoming. Reporters wrote that Calamity was youthful and pretty, and that she and Wild Bill were both dressed in buckskins with long fringe, white stetsons, and clean boots. Calamity, described as an "Amazonian woman of the frontier," waved and yelled at all the excited prospectors crowding Deadwood's narrow, winding main street. No wonder [that] 190-person wagon train powered by ox-teams stopped the traffic in the gold camp.

Calamity and Wild Bill weren't the only attractions. It was an historic occasion: the first whores had arrived in Deadwood, riding on their wagons like queens greeting the cheering male populace. Two experienced madams and faro dealers, Madam Mustachio and Madam Dirty Em, soon set up brothels in what quickly became a thriving red-light district that lasted for over 100 years in Deadwood.

During that wild summer of 1876, Calamity made Deadwood, Dakota Territory, her headquarters because "Sin City" had the most action-brawls and shootings, saloons and hurdy-gurdy houses, roistering gold-seekers and professional gamblers. She swaggered into the bars ordering "Give me a shot of booze and slop her over the brim."

Sometimes, she provided free entertainment to anyone who would listen by telling fantastic tales of her exploits, like robbing stagecoaches and fighting Indians, with herself in the chief male role. And when Calamity got drunk, watch out!

Madam DuFran, her friend and frequent employer, wrote: "She even had a band of coyotes beat for howling when she was drunk and that was most of the time. The Hills reverberated to the wild howling of Calamity Jane, the untamed woman of the wild, wild west."

This untamed woman certainly got around the frontier. In Cheyenne, WY, she shot out the lights in a saloon; in Miles City, MT, she was arrested for brawling, and it took three strong men to drag her to jail, no doubt howling all the way.

Every town in the Black Hills knew her well. In Rapid City, whooping and hollering, she rode a red bull up main street to the delight of the onlookers. In Hot Springs, she was blasted in the newspaper for putting on a "drunken exhibition of horsemanship and shooting." In a Deadwood theater, she strode up to the footlights and spit tobacco juice all over the leading lady's gown.

The following news items appeared February 8, 1879, in the *Black Hills Daily Times*: "It is reported from Sturgis City that Calamity Jane walloped two women at that place yesterday. Calamity can get away with half a dozen ordinary pugilistic women when she turns loose, but she never fights unless she is in the right, and then she is not backward to tackle even a masculine shoulder hitter."

Understandably, once a person had an encounter with Calamity Jane, that person never forgot her. Her bizarre behavior and escapades in the border country always made for fascinating conversation and lively reading. Calamity Jane was news.

During the summer of 1876, Calamity Jane followed Wild Bill Hickok around like a puppy, but the elegant Kansas marshal had no time for this vulgar woman, being a newly married man who spent his time writing loving letters to his bride, prospecting for gold, and gambling. Calamity did her best to spread the gossip that there was a romance between them, but few believed her.

After Wild Bill was shot in the back during a poker game in the Saloon No. 10, Calamity later bragged that she was the one who had captured the assassin, Jack McCall, in Shoudy's meat market with a meat cleaver. But this was another lie, according to many witnesses of the murder.

Calamity did set herself up as the chief mourner of Wild Bill, wailing and crying while the motley gang of the gold camp filed through the tent where the handsome corpse was laid out. Even though she behaved like a bereaved sweetheart of the dead man, she didn't fool anybody.

However, there definitely was another side to the roughneck Calamity—a kind, tender, caring side. Her contemporaries agree that she was an angel of mercy to the sick. She frequently helped nurse the sick with Dr. L. F. Babcock, an early Deadwood doctor, who praised her as "beautiful and brave" for her nursing work.

During the terrible small pox epidemic of 1878, it was Calamity who nursed a great many contagious patients. According to Madam DuFran, Calamity had small pox when she was a youngster and was thus immune.

Nevertheless, it was a remarkable act of mercy, day after day, week after week, to care for the small pox victims in filthy tents and shacks with no running water or sanitary conveniences of any kind. The only medicines were epsom salts and cream of tartar.

Madam DuFran related how Calamity volunteered to nurse eight sick men who were quarantined with small pox in a shack on White Rocks mountain above Deadwood. Probably because of her ministrations, five of her patients survived.

When a patient died, Calamity wrapped him in a blanket and [carried him] down the mountain for someone to dig another grave. Then she conducted the burial rites and recited the only prayer she knew, "Now I Lay Me Down to Sleep."

During the small pox epidemic, Calamity Jane was much more than a nurse: she was a doctor, cook, chambermaid, water boy, under-taker, sexton, and preacher. Brown and Willard, two authors who knew Calamity, summarized her nursing activities in their book *Black Hills Trails:* "It made no difference to her that she knew them not, or that no gold would be there to repay her for the labor, the sacrifice, the danger. They were fellow beings in distress and needed help."

No wonder contemporary writers labeled Calamity Jane as "The West's Joan of Arc," "The Black Hills' Florence Nightengale," and "Lady Robin Hood."

The basic plot of the Lady Robin Hood story is that a penniless Calamity pulled a gun on a storekeeper to get groceries for a sick fam-ily who couldn't afford to buy food. Probably the storekeeper would have let her charge if she had asked politely. But Calamity always thought it was fun to wave a gun around. She consistently performed with showmanship with an eye to the audience. Maybe even with an eye on posterity—who knows.

Calamity left Deadwood in 1880 and for about fifteen years roamed the frontier playing her many roles. In 1898, an aging and weather-beaten Calamity Jane returned to Deadwood with a little girl in tow, announcing that she was married to Clinton Burke, a hack driver, and claiming the little girl was hers. The child was actu-ally Burke's stepdaughter. Although Calamity claimed to have been married many times—and there were many men who claimed to have been her husband—there is no record or proof of her ever being legally married to anybody.

At last she got a job where she could show off, with Kohl and Middleton, an amusement company which traveled in eastern cities. She was billed as "The Famous Woman Scout of the Wild West and Heroine of a Thousand Thrilling Adventures." Although the aging tomboy could still shoot amazingly well, she was fired for excessive drinking and for her shocking language.

Back in Deadwood, Calamity lashed out at people who tried to reform her: "Why don't the sons of bitches leave me alone and let me go to hell my own route?"

Calamity Jane died of alcoholism in the little mining town of Terry, a few miles from Deadwood, on August 11, 1903, age about fifty-three years.

Newspapers reported another of the "largest funerals Deadwood has ever seen." A showperson to the last, she had made a dying request: "Bury me beside Wild Bill, the only man I ever loved." So she was.

And now the two graves, side by side in Mount Moriah cemetery, are Deadwood's most popular tourist attraction. In death, she is closer to Wild Bill than she ever was in life. Many observers report that Wild Bill has been spinning in his grave ever since she caught up with him.

How did Calamity Jane become so famous?

One reason is that everyone who knew this colorful woman inevitably had at least two stories to tell about her: one about the picturesque bad side and the other about her humanitarian side, her generosity and her nursing of suffering pioneers. These stories, often embellished with each telling, were handed down from generation to generation, especially in the Black Hills, which has always lovingly claimed her as its own.

Another reason for her notoriety is that in 1885, seventeen years before her death, author Edward Wheeler whose pseudonym was Ned Buntline, used her name for a fictional heroine of numerous dime novels with a western setting and featuring well-known western characters. *Calamity Jane, The Heroine of Whoop-Up,* was the title of one best seller.

Over and over again, Calamity Jane was mentioned in many diaries, sketches, and newspapers of the gold rush days and later. When the first authors began writing Black Hills history books, they always included a chapter on Calamity Jane. She was good copy.

In the twentieth century, the motion picture industry discovered Calamity Jane and glamorized her life while dramatizing that make-believe romance between Calamity and Wild Bill Hickok. Bearing no resemblance whatever to the original, actresses like Doris Day and Jane Russell portrayed plain Jane in fictional situations. But no matter—her fame grew.

Calamity Jane had always been a red-hot publicity hound. How she would have loved all the attention she has received from the media in the twentieth century. She would have enjoyed the publicity about being "Queen of the Wild West" and a "prostitute with a heart of gold."

How does one assess the contributions of this complex, masculine woman? Has she received more attention than she deserves? Why is she so unforgettable?

Her friend, Madam Dora DuFran, suggests the answer: "Calamity Jane was truly a Diamond in the Rough."

PART III

PIONEERS AND PERSONALITIES

Every village and hamlet has a history laced with those who didn't wait for others, of individuals of sturdy stock and independent disposition who led their compatriots into an uncertain future. In this, Deadwood is no different.

In the following excerpts culled from a variety of times and sources, we examine a cast of characters as rich as any in the West. From Jedediah Smith, purportedly the first white man to traverse many areas of the vast frontier, to Aunt Sally, Custer's cook and arguably the first non–Native American woman to trek to the Black Hills, each has a story that, together, transformed a region.

"Firsts—Explorers, Cooks & Teachers"
from *Tales of the Black Hills*
Helen Rezatto
1983

In her entertaining collection of vignettes tied to the settlement of the Black Hills, author Helen Rezatto wrote of the non-Native men and women who first trod the Black Hills of Dakota Territory. In the following chapters, taken from Rezatto's book Tales of the Black Hills, *we learn of the region's early day explorers, a black cook who accompanied Custer's expedition, and a teacher who sought her own frontier in the Black Hills.*

Jedediah Smith—First White Man in the Black Hills

An impressive mural in the South Dakota state capitol building at Pierre depicts a large keelboat, the "Yellowstone," floating on the Missouri River. In the center of the painting are figures of fur traders and trappers in the prow with the focus on a man kneeling in prayer. It was "a powerful prayer that moved us all greatly," reported Hugh Glass, one of the listeners.

The man delivering the prayer is Jedediah Smith, Bible-toting fur-trader and trail-blazer, who asked the Lord's blessing for the dead and wounded after the Ashley party had a fight with the Arikara Indians. Smith's celebrated prayer became known as the first recorded act of Christian worship in the land that is now South Dakota.

Jedediah Smith was born in New York state in 1799 where he received an education suitable for a teacher or a minister. As a boy, he read the journals of Lewis and Clark, which stimulated him to seek adventure and fortune in the unknown and beckoning west.

When a young man, he traveled to St. Louis, the bustling frontier town where the boats of the fur traders and adventurers crowded the Missouri River. A strapping six-footer, Smith, at age 23, joined General William Ashley's second fur-trading expedition. He was a devout Methodist, prayed every day, and carried his Bible with him wherever he went in the uncharted wilderness.

After the Arikara fight, Jed Smith volunteered to carry the news of the battle to Ashley's partner on the Yellowstone River. General Ashley was so impressed with the young volunteer's bravery and the speed with which he accomplished the arduous mission that he made Smith a captain.

In the early fall of 1823, Captain Jed Smith led a party of fifteen men from Fort Kiowa on the Missouri River (near present-day Chamberlain, SD) across the plains to the southern Black Hills, their destination being the Wind River country of Wyoming.

While traveling through or near the southern Black Hills searching for water and respite from the heat, they were trudging single file through plum and chokecherry thickets. Then without warning, a grizzly bear sprang out of the brush, knocking Jed to the ground, and the animal's claws almost tore off the man's entire scalp and left his ear dangling. The other men managed to shoot the bear.

Although prostrate and wounded, Jed was able to coolly give instructions to his stunned comrades, especially to James Clyman, whom he asked to get out his emergency kit and begin sewing the scalp back into place. Clyman cut away the blood-matted hair and clumsily did as he was told. Although Clyman said he could do nothing for the mangled ear, Jed Smith ordered, "Try!" Clyman did. The crude surgery worked, and in ten days Jed had recovered enough to mount his horse and keep riding west.

Jed Smith usually kept a diary full of observations about the natural history seen on his travels, but on this trip he did not, perhaps because of his injuries.

Fortunately, there is a written record. James Clyman, who had saved Smith's life, many years later wrote an account of this trek

Ramshackle construction and ever-present mud were signatures of early-day Deadwood, as depicted in this 1877 stereopticon photograph. (Photo courtesy of Adams Museum, Deadwood, SD)

from the Missouri River through the southern Black Hills and into Wyoming. Historians have analyzed Clyman's vague descriptions of the terrain, rivers and landmarks and have come up with at least three different conclusions of the routes the Jed Smith party took. Did they follow the White River and then cut over to French Creek? Or did they cross the south fork of the Cheyenne River in the southern Hills, probably near the present location of Hot Springs and Edgemont with perhaps an entanglement in Hells Canyon? However, most readers of the Clyman report believe that from whichever direction they came, Jed Smith and his men passed through the Buffalo Gap break into the Black Hills.

Clyman recalled in his report that when they arrived in the Black Hills, "We entered a pleasant undulating pine Region cool and refreshing so different from the hot dusty planes." This was to be an oft-repeated reaction of many explorers to follow.

From this Clyman report also comes the story told by a Moses Harris which has been the source for some colorful folklore about the wonders of the Black Hills. Harris claimed that he had seen a petrified forest with trees, branches and leaves all turned to stone, "wild cherries peetrified into rubies of reddest hue and peetrified birds a-sittin' on the branches of a tree a-singin' peetrified songs." Perhaps Harris, who publicized this tall tale around many campfires, had been drinking wine in the petrified forest north of what is now Edgemont, SD.

Jedediah Smith, throughout his short, active life, proved himself to be a leader with great endurance and determination, and ranged over the entire western United States. He and two others, William Sublette and George Jackson, eventually purchased the productive Ashley fur business and did well with their venture, trapping beaver, muskrat and all kinds of fur-bearing animals in the wild country.

Smith frequently sent money home to his parents and to his younger brothers for their education. In this letter to his brother, he reveals his religious beliefs: "As it respects my welfare, I hardly durst speak. I find myself one of the most ungrateful, unthankful creatures imaginable. O, when shall I be under the care of a Christian Church! I have need of your prayers. I wish our Society to bear up to a Throne of Grace." No wonder Smith was regarded as a true Christian.

In 1831, while scouting alone for water for his wagon train on the Santa Fe trail, a hunting party of Comanches killed the 32-year-old Smith on the Cimarron River in southern Kansas. His body was never recovered and details of his death were later learned from the Indians. Reportedly, his distinctive silver pistols turned up in Mexican pawn shops.

During his brief lifetime, Smith had made a remarkable record as an explorer and trail-blazer. He made the first complete exploration of the South Pass in Wyoming, later the gateway to the far west used by the emigrants in their covered wagons. He was the first American to cross the Sierra Nevada mountains into California. He was the first white man to explore the entire Pacific coast from Canada to Mexico.

Throughout his years on the frontier, this Christian man had consistently opposed giving or selling liquor to the Indians. An official national law, enacted in his memory in June, 1832, prohibited traffic in intoxicants in Indian territory.

Today, South Dakotans honor Jedediah Smith because he was the first white man to enter the Black Hills. Although there were no navigable rivers to attract the fur trade, the Black Hills, from time immemorial, were destined to bewitch several races of people with their charms, both real and fabled.

Sarah Campbell—First Non-Indian Woman in the Black Hills

Sarah Campbell, a Negro, was the only woman with the Custer Expedition of 1874, which had been commissioned by the United States government to explore the Black Hills and to check up on the rumors of gold in this mysterious and unknown region. "Aunt Sally"—as the men called her—was cook for John Smith, the sutler for the expedition. She was thus the first non-Indian woman, white or black, to see the Black Hills.

Aunt Sally was probably just as delighted as were the men—many of whom recorded their reactions in diaries, letters, military reports, and newspaper accounts—to discover that the Black Hills were really not black and gloomy as they appeared from a distance; instead the mountains were covered with thick, green pine forests which made them look dark; and they were full of marvelous surprises—sparkling streams, flower-fill meadows, painted canyons—a cool, welcome paradise after the hot alkaline northern Dakota plains and their ever-present hordes of mosquitoes and swarms of grasshoppers.

Probably, Aunt Sally rode in the sutler's wagon which, like all the wagons, was pulled by a team of six mules and driven by a whip-cracking, profane driver. As likely as not, Aunt Sally, being the only woman in this summer wilderness trek, must have had numerous problems involving her own privacy and meager comforts.

Aunt Sally's job was to cook for civilian John Smith, the post trader commonly called "sutler," who accompanied the expedition and sold whiskey, food, and other special provisions to the soldiers.

Presumably, Aunt Sally was expected to exercise her ingenuity to create culinary treats he could sell. The government rations included hard tack, bacon, rio coffee, rice, sugar, vinegar, salt and pepper, supplemented by occasional fresh beef from the herd with the expedition and occasional venison from the antelope and deer the men shot along the way.

There is no record of how ingenious Aunt Sally was in concocting appetizing meals from the frugal supplies or whether she could make soup out of stones. The routine procedure called for the cooks to respond to the first reveille at 2:35 a.m. and to begin unloading the mess gear kept in the big chests in the wagons, to build fires, and to begin preparing breakfast.

One wishes Aunt Sally had been able to record her feelings, but no doubt she enjoyed the myriad charms of the Black Hills as much as did the eloquent observers whose reactions are preserved in writing about the spectacular scenery, the cool weather, and the delightful band music echoing from peak to peak.

At French Creek, near the present town of Custer, SD, Horatio Ross, an experienced miner with the Custer Expedition, made the historic gold discovery. Then everyone went wild digging and scratching and panning gold with shovels, knives, picks—any available implement—whether a mule-whacker or a scientist or a sutler's black cook.

William Curtis, the 23-year-old star reporter for the *Chicago Inter-Ocean* and the *New York World* reported the gold discovery at French Creek. In the same issue in which the momentous gold discovery in the Black Hills was announced to the country is published his exclusive interview with Aunt Sally, in the August 27, 1874, issue of the *Chicago Inter-Ocean:*

> *The most excited contestant in this chase after fortune was "Aunt Sally," the sutler's colored cook, a huge mountain of dusky flesh, and "the first white woman [actually, the first non–Native American woman] that ever saw the Black Hills," as she frequently says. She is an old frontiersman, as it were, having been*

up and down the Missouri ever since its muddy water was broken by a paddle wheel, and having accumulated quite a little property, had settled down in Bismarck to ease and luxury.

"Money didn't done brung dis chile out hyar, now, I tells ye dat; dis hain't no common nigger, now I tells ye: not it ain't, now hyar me; and ye wouldn't cotch dis gal totin' chuck out hyar now, I tells ye, if it haadn't bin for seein' dese hyar Black Hills dat Custer fetched us to. I'se heered 'bout dese here hills long 'fore Custer did. Now I'm talkin'. When I was on de Missouri—cooked on first boat dat ever run up dat stream, an' I hain't had no hard luck, neither, now I tells ye folks. But I wanted to see dese Black Hills—an' dey ain't no blacker dan I am and I'm no African, now you just bet I ain't; I'm none of yer common herd, I've got the money to back it, now I have, I tell you."

Aunt Sally's Dream of Gold

Aunt Sally expected to find the Black Hills in some indefinite way or other adapted to the colored race, and was terribly disappointed; but the gold discoveries compensated for the lack of any distinctive mark of her race, and she joined in the development with religious fervor. She talked incessantly about them from morning to night, and when she packed her mammoth body into a little wagon that provided for her and her "traps," her dreams were of gold mines, and "'ery thing dats on his dis hyar earth, now I know." She went to the stream when the strike was made, "scratched gravel," and staked out her claim, and she says she's coming here as soon as anybody, "now you hyar me."

Aunt Sally, along with the rest of the miners, experienced and inexperienced, staked out her illegal claim, recorded as "No. 7 Below Discovery." Later, these claims in Indian Territory were probably taken over by more prospectors who unlawfully invaded the region within the next year.

Whether or not Aunt Sally had a hand in trying to tenderize and cook the tough bear meat provided by General Custer for the officers' mess, it is probably safe to assume that she became an expert at cooking the plentiful venison. One can easily visualize huge Aunt Sally in a covered wagon, loaded with rattling pots and pans, jouncing over the pine-clad mountains and rocky outcroppings and emerald meadows, and driven by a teamster swearing at the balky mules.

According to the Curtis interview, from the time Aunt Sally was the first excited female tourist in the Black Hills and then participated in the French Creek discovery, she was determined to return. Gold! That was the magnet that attracted her—as well as thousands of other gold-seekers.

Aunt Sally kept her vow and return she did, but there is no conclusive record of just when. Several reports state that she walked beside an ox-drawn wagon train from Bismarck to the Black Hills, establishing herself first at Crook City, then at Galena, cooking and midwifing for various families. There is no record of whether she ever returned to the French Creek area to check on "No. 7 Below Discovery." Eventually, she filed a claim at Elk Creek near Roubaix in Lawrence County and lived on a little ranch there.

Rumors and contradictions abound concerning Aunt Sally. Some old-timers reported that she claimed her father had been a Cherokee Indian and her mother a Negro, that she and her mother had spent the Civil War years in Canada until Custer sent her money to return to the United States.

Aunt Sally also claimed that she was a personal cook both for General Custer and for Captain Miles Keogh, the owner of Comanche, the famous horse who survived the Battle of the Little Big Horn. Although it is possible that, at various times, she may have cooked for these officers, there is no record of it.

Several sons and daughters of Galena pioneers, the old silver-mining town, remember stories their parents told and retold about popular Aunt Sally whom they loved and respected. How she enjoyed relating colorful anecdotes about her adventures with the Custer Expedition, while puffing on her pipe, her ample sides shaking with merriment. The main character in all her tales was her hero, George Armstrong Custer. She had the reputation of being a good midwife, a superb cook, and a lover of children.

An unusual aspect of Aunt Sally's life was that she found a hungry, ragged 10-year-old white orphan boy crying on the streets of Deadwood. She took him home and adopted him as her son. His name was Anthony Herr or Wier. He never smiled so she called him "Sad."

Aunt Sally, who was her own best press agent, lived happily among other pioneers in the Black Hills, mostly white people who settled Crook City, Galena, Elk Creek, and Roubaix areas—all in Lawrence County, South Dakota.

She died on April 13, 1888, at age 73 or 75, and two Deadwood newspapers published complimentary obituaries. *The Deadwood Daily Pioneer* concluded: "Everybody knew her, everybody liked her, and not a few will learn with deep regret that death has claimed her."

She was buried on Vinegar Hill, a beautiful little mountain cemetery in the tall pines west of Galena. Seth Galvin, a Galena native who knew her as a boy and wrote about her in his unpublished memoirs, kept her grave in good condition. He placed the first simple wooden marker on which was carved: "Aunt Sally—First Woman in the Black Hills," which is now displayed in the Adams Museum in Deadwood.

Mr. Galvin's interpretation of why Aunt Sally always said she was the first white woman in the Black Hills was this: "She was not very literate, and the term 'white' was the only [term] she knew. She meant 'civilized.'"

In 1934, Seth Galvin enlisted the aid of Fred Borsch, another Galena native, and the two men built a simple wooden fence around Aunt Sally's grave to keep out wandering cattle and erected a larger and improved marker.

The name of Sarah Campbell will live forever in Black Hills history; for as her grave marker says, "She Ventured with the Vanguard of Civilization."

Likewise, the name of "Aunt Sally," a wonderful friend and neighbor to many, lives on in the long memories of the sons and daughters, even the grandchildren, of the pioneers of Lawrence County in the Black Hills of South Dakota.

Annie Tallent—First White Woman in the Black Hills

Annie Tallent was the first white woman to enter the Black Hills, and ever since she has been honored and revered for this "first" in addition to other accomplishments of a more uncontroversial nature. At age 47, she was the only woman with the 28-member Russell-Collins or Gordon Party, as it is variously called. These gold-seekers made secret preparations in Sioux City, Iowa, for their trek to the Black Hills in 1874, violating both the Laramie Treaty of 1868 and the express orders of the United States government not to invade them, for the Black Hills were supposed to be strictly off limits to whites.

Annie Tallent was born in New York state, was educated in a female seminary, and eventually moved westward. She married David Tallent, a lawyer, and it was with him and their nine-year-old son Robert that she embarked on her perilous and celebrated march to the forbidden El Dorado.

Twenty-five years later Mrs. Tallent wrote the Bible of regional histories, *The Black Hills or Last Hunting Grounds of the Dacotahs,* in which she described the adventures and hardships of the perilous 78-day journey to the Black Hills when she walked mile after mile beside the heavily loaded wagon train into Indian Territory.

Constantly tormented by visions of the scalping knife, she described a hazardous journey across the barren plains in late fall, the arguments among the disgruntled men, the desolation of the Badlands, and the practical reason for tying gunny sacks around her worn shoes which was to protect her feet from the cold.

In vivid detail, she recalled how the first glimpse of the shadowy Black Hills and of the Bear Butte landmark "guarding the entrance to the unknown land" made every heart sing "paeans of joy and thankfulness." Despite the wintry weather, the heartened group finally located the Custer wagon trail out of the Black Hills and noted traces of civilization such as a few kernels of corn and discarded army gear. At this point, Annie Tallent confessed that she sat down on a log and cried from sheer homesickness.

By backtracking Custer's route, made five months earlier, the party arrived on French Creek near the present site of Custer city on December 23rd in heavy snow. They spent a miserable Christmas, dreaming of home, and eating "coarse everyday fare" not turkey and plum puddings. A forest of Christmas trees surrounded them, but there were no decorations—"nothing but picks, shovels, gold pans, and an ox chain for ornamentation," wrote Mrs. Tallent.

Except for listing the individual members of the group at the beginning of her book, the author never mentions the presence of her husband and little boy throughout the entire ordeal. However, the men soon began constructing seven cabins inside the famous Gordon Stockade while hoping for reinforcements and praying not to be discovered by the military contingents they knew were searching for violators of the law.

About a month later, United States Army officers arrested the trespassers and escorted the unhappy group to Fort Laramie, WY, where they were all released without punishment. Annie Tallent rode a government mule out of the Black Hills; thus she was the first woman to enter and to exit.

But it wasn't long before the United States government and the relieved army patrols gave up trying to stop the Black Hills Gold Rush as thousands of fortune-hunters began pouring into the Indian reservation from all directions.

Not until 1876 did the Tallents return to the Black Hills where they settled first in Custer, then in Deadwood, and finally in Rapid City. David Tallent eventually deserted his family and disappeared from the region. Mrs. Tallent, ever resourceful and self-sufficient, taught school in log schoolhouses at Tigerville and Hill City, then became postmistress and teacher at Rochford. Always interested in education, she served as superintendent of public instruction in Pennington County, proving herself [to] be an active community leader and church worker wherever she lived.

Annie Tallent spent her final years living with her son Robert in Sturgis where she researched and wrote her book. Her chronicle includes detailed histories of all the Black Hills settlements, accounts of mines and other industries, sketches of prominent people, including Wild Bill Hickok, who she thought looked like a Quaker minister instead of a gunman. She wrote colorful descriptions of memorable events like the devastating Deadwood fire of 1879. Included are lengthy, dramatized narratives of the Battle of the Little Big Horn and the Wounded Knee uprising; however, she provides few sources for most of the voluminous information presented on a variety of subjects.

In her history book, Mrs. Tallent writes at length about the Custer Expedition of 1874, but she does not state that Sarah Campbell, or "Aunt Sally"—as she was called—a cook with the expedition, was the first non-Indian woman to visit the Hills. Her only mention of the Negress is in this context: "Aunt Sally, who claimed the distinction of being 'de fustest culled lady in the Brack Hills,' was one of the early settlers of Crook City." Whether or not Mrs. Tallent felt any rivalry with Aunt Sally about who had the prior claim, white or "culled," she does not elaborate.

Mrs. Tallent's attitude toward Indians reflected the white attitude of that era: the Indians were savages and "the only good Indian was a dead one." Definitely, she suggests that their legal rights to a rich land coveted by the greedy whites should not have been taken seriously and that "a long list of fancied wrongs, treasured up for years" contributed to the bitter hostilities, resulting in the crowning tragedy of the Little Big Horn.

In 1974, Brevet Press published the second edition of the Tallent history with a special introduction by Virginia Driving Hawk Sneve, a Brule Sioux Indian, who is a teacher, writer, and editor. Mrs. Sneve strongly objects to many of the book's discussions of Indian life and beliefs, including the author's biased reporting of the conflicts between Indians and whites. Mrs. Sneve believes that "Annie Tallent's malicious, bigoted treatment of the Dakota or Sioux Indians, would best serve mankind if it were burned rather than reprinted in this edition to continue to perpetuate a distorted, untrue portrait of the American Indian."

However, in the white world Annie Tallent is a favorite heroine, hailed—the personification of the ideal pioneer woman. Many schools and prestigious awards have been named in her honor. The Society of Black Hills Pioneers erected, near the town of Custer, a statue dedicated to her memory with the inscription: "The world is better because she lived and worked in it."

When Annie Tallent died in 1901, aged 74, in Sturgis, SD, she was reported to have been given the most impressive funeral ever held in the history of the Society of Black Hills Pioneers. She was buried in a family plot at Elgin, Illinois.

In arriving at a fair assessment of Annie Tallent's contributions to development of the Black Hills and the significance and influence of her book, historians would do well to recall the words of a writer named Froude: "To be entirely just in our estimate of other ages is not only difficult, but is impossible."

"THE MYSTERY MAN," TOM MOORE
FROM ADAMS MUSEUM
FRANK B. BRYANT
CIRCA 1930 (?)

Dictated in the eighth decade of Frank B. Bryant's life, the follow-ing account describes one of the unsung heroes who helped settle the Black Hills in the 1870s. Though the exploits of Tom Moore didn't gen-erate any dime novels, and therefore didn't create a lingering legend, before he died Frank Bryant wanted to preserve for "the record" some mention of one of the faceless men who toiled to make a living in an often unforgiving land.

In cowboy parlance, Tom Moore wore the proverbial white hat, stood up for those less fortunate, did not long suffer fools, and could shoot as well as anyone in the West. The Civil War vet had come west with the throng of miners, muleskinners, and madams who all were in search of their private El Dorado. Moore hunted bear with a smirk, bedded down with black prospectors when he wanted to make a point, and wasn't afraid to administer a bit of frontier justice when it was warranted. Here then is Frank Bryant's account of one man's legacy.

The Mystery Man
The following is a brief account of an outstanding character in the early history of the Black Hills. He was known to all of the old-timers in the Black Hills and elsewhere in the West. His name was Tom Moore.

I am eighty years old. I have spent my lifetime as a mining engi-neer in mining camps of the West. In every camp, without exception, I have found an old pioneer who knew him or had heard of him. The reports were always the same; they all knew what he could do and would do with that terrible fifty caliber Needle Gun.

A man in his early forties, five feet ten inches tall, blue eyes, black curly hair, a moustache, and weighing around one hundred sixty pounds. He was not addicted to either liquor or cards. He had some education as I have related in my account of the trip of the Bryant Party into the Black Hills in 1875. Nothing was known of his antecedents. He did say that he had been with Grant as a sharpshooter at Missionary Ridge.

Tom spoke sign language fluently and a smattering of several Indian languages. He was interpreter on the Rosebud Indian Reservation at the time of his death. I don't have the date nor his age. I never saw his name in print.

Tom Moore was one of the many men who have made their contribution to opening the Missouri River Basin and passed into history, unsung and forgotten. I feel that some record should be left of this outstanding character.

Stories of him were legion. I append a few of the ones I remember and those given me by others.

A party of Negroe (sic) prospectors came into Deadwood in 1876. Immediately the roughnecks began talking of running the black SOB's out, of throwing them and their stuff into the creek. Moore threw his bed roll down with the colored men's duffel and ended all talk of disturbing them. This was the party of Negroes who discovered the Nigger Hill diggings on the western slope of the Black Hills.

The first fall of snow in the fall of 1875 incited Tom and George Hauser to go hunting below Deadwood. The snow, three or four inches deep, was just right for tracking. A couple of miles below town they struck the tracks of a big bear. The size of his tracks indicated he was a full grown Jo Dandy. Tom examined the tracks carefully and observed, "real fresh." He suggested they follow the tracks to see how big the varmit (sic) really was. George knew the portent of such talk and protested that he wasn't hunting bear, he was hunting deer or elk. Tom persisted but George wasn't a bear hunter. He said, "Tom, I know that you are a hell of a good shot and I know of your courage, but just remember that we are one hundred sixty miles from a Doctor. Forget that dam (sic) bear and let's get us a deer or an elk."

Moore insisted they have a look at the bear. The tracks led along the hillside and down into a cave where he had probably decided to winter. Tom looked down at the cave and called, "Here he is, George."

"If you are dam (sic) fool enough, Tom, to monkey with a big bear, give me time to climb this tree," which was a tall spruce and would have suited Hauser just fine if it had been twice as tall. Tom roared down the cave, "Good morning, Mr. Bear, how you wintering?" Nothing but a deep menacing growl in return. Moore calls to Bruin with the same answers. He set his gun down and rustled a big boulder, and rolled it down on the bear. It came out boiling mad, growling and barking as he sat up in front of Tom who cut him a sharp military salute and said, "Good morning, sir." This pantomime continued for several minutes until the brute started to lower for the charge when Tom fired and killed him. Tom reloaded quickly and stood at the ready.

Deciding the varmint was dead, he called to George, "Don't that beat Hell, I salute him, fire once for rank and here he is dead. Come on down and let's see if he is fat." Fat he was much to Hauser's glee as he needed bear grease for his curly locks. "He is all yours, George, I've had my fun," the hunter informed his partner and resumed his hunt for good meat. Every old-timer knew the story of Moore and the bear.

The details of the two following anecdotes were given me by Judge John E. Wasson. He witnessed the first episode and was a party to the second.

A preacher named Smith arrived in Deadwood in 1876 to work with the miners. The Evangelist had a very successful three months stay in the camp. It was so fruitful that he determined to carry his campaign for Christ into the mining camps of Montana. He, with a companion, went up Deadwood Gulch to the mouth of Blacktail, followed it to the False Bottom divide and continued on down that creek.

A short distance below old Garden City, the two were ambushed by Indians and Smith (was) killed. His escort fired once and downed a Redskin and then broke for Deadwood. A posse was quickly organized to overtake and punish the red devils. The Indian, shot in the ambush, was badly wounded. He dragged himself to a tree, got his back against it, lifted his knees and layed (sic) his gun between them, awaiting the inevitable return of the whitemen. He must have hoped the man who had shot him would be the leader. He reasoned correctly, but his aim was poor. He shot and raised to his knees with a mighty whoop, and of course was riddled with bullets. The posse scoured the country but found no Indians. Returning to town, the man who had wounded the Indian stopped and cut off the head and tied it to his saddle.

Back in Deadwood, the first order of the day was to quench their thirst. All day without a drink was Sahara itself. The man with the trophy, heated to combustion with "Tiger Sweat," climbed aboard his horse and chased up and down the street lashing his horse with the Indian head. No one said a word. Moore, who hadn't been with the posse, came out, saw what was going on and walked out into the street and intercepted the wild man. Tom dragged him from his horse, hit him with a vicious slap across the mouth with his open hand, and commanded the cur, "Go bury that head, do you hear me! Bury it deep you yellow livered sob and get about it right now." The skunk slipped away and did as he had been bid.

Tom Moore had a saloon in Bismarck, Dakota Territory in 1873. John E. Wasson, a veteran of the 41st regiment of New York, was candidate for County Attorney in that County's first election. John was a Democrat by "Religion." The Northern Pacific railroad was just built into the city, (and) it was really tough. A company of soldiers were stationed there for the dual purpose of keeping the Indians from running off the contractors' stock, and to prevent the whites from killing one another. Wasson was popular notwithstanding he was a Democrat, and this was but eight years since the conflict ended.

As election day approached, his Republican opponent became fearful of the outcome and informed the Commandent (sic) of his predicament and asked for help. The Soldier told him not to worry, that if need be he would vote the troops. The veteran hearing of this asked Moore for advice. Tom told Wasson, "That Shavetail won't vote those soldiers." The news of the Saloon Man's position reached the officer.

He sent for Tom. He reacted typically, "To hell with him, I'm no soldier. If he wants to see me let him come to my place of business. He knows where I live." The Lieutenant came into Tom's saloon, introduced himself and inquired if it was true that Moore opposed voting the troops. His reply was right to the point, "Soldier, you aren't voting your troops." "Very well," returned the officer, (who) turned on his heel and walked out. Wasson won hands down. It was very apparent the Officer knew Moore's prerogatives.

Frank Sage knew Tom on the Union Pacific before he went to Bismarck. He was trading horses. Horse thieves were active and bold. Moore lost no horses to the thieves. If he missed a horse he went after it. He often saw stock belonging to others. When asked why he didn't bring the animals in, his laconic answer was, "Why didn't you come along?"

Abe Jones and Tom had a coal mine near the present Belle Fourche. They had a disagreement. Abe had Moore arrested and thrown in a log jail. Tom set the jail on fire. Someone noted smoke pouring from the Bastile (sic) and rushed to notify the deputy sheriff. He found Tom lying on his belly with his mouth to the crack under the door. Since there was no other place in which to confine him, he was turned loose on his own cognizance.

Charley Francis and Tom were hunting on lower Whitewood. Returning after dark they saw the reflection of a fire on the dead cottonwoods along the creek below them. They cached their horses and climbed down to reconnoiter. They recognized the campers as members of Blackburn's gang of road agents. The hunters rushed into Deadwood to inform the sheriff of their discovery. They proposed that he get three others and the six would go back and bring in the outlaws. The Law Man thought differently. He organized a posse. Immediately the reflected light of the campfire was sighted and they opened fire. The road agents returned a few shots and hitailed (sic) it out of there. Moore and Francis were mad and disgusted. Tom suggested it offered a good opportunity to dispose of a sheriff, but passed it up.

Francis owned a bank in Sturgis afterwards.

Moore had known Wild Bill somewhere. There was recognition, but no hand shakes. It was the same with Wyatt Earp. Buffalo hunters were an anathema to him. In his book they were as low as they could get, lacking honor or integrity completely.

In the literature, Calamity Jane and Wild Bill Hickok are always linked together as contemporaries. I think research will reveal that Wild Bill Hickok and Calamity Jane never knew one another in the Hills. Wild Bill was killed on August 2nd, 1876 and Calamity Jane came in the fall with a freight outfit.

I think these items of history are relevant and should be in the record.

"A Little Girl in Deadwood"
from *Old Deadwood Days*
Estelline Bennett
1928

*In its infancy, through adolescence and middle age, Deadwood tended
to attract the great and the gritty, the dignified and the decadent.
Some would argue it still does so today. But, at its inception were the
innate hunger for gold and all it could buy, coupled with the legendary lure of a place few had ever been—a wilderness known as the
Black Hills of Dakota Territory.*

*Though its birth in the summer of 1876 was anything but pretty,
Deadwood's adolescence was attended by the sounds of pounding hammers, howling saloons, eager merchants, and muleskinners shouting
their ox teams through a sea of endless mud in a town not yet tamed.*

*Horse thieves, road agents, claim jumpers, and even a few bad
characters rode the rip-roaring wave that cascaded into Deadwood
Gulch. In their wake, like a good wagon following a bad horse,
came the law.*

*Just a year after the first prospectors tumbled into what would
become one of the richest gold strikes anywhere, Federal Judge
Granville G. Bennett moved to Deadwood with his family in 1877. His
young daughter, Estelline, would grow up with the town and provide
one set of the "unslumbering eyes" that watched all and acknowledged
little, yet retained such simple reminiscences for a wonderful book she
called* Old Deadwood Days. *In her work, Estelline Bennett captures
a bit of normalcy in a decidedly unusual place, a town of neighbor-
hoods and back alleys, hurdy-gurdy houses and honky-tonks, steep
stairways, church services, and the sounds of the arriving stage. Here,
then, is the account of one little girl in a thriving gold camp named
Deadwood.*

As a young woman, Estelline Bennett lived in the first row of houses above Deadwood's Bad Lands, affording her a view and colorful memories of the raucous activities that occurred down in the notorious den. (Photo courtesy of the Adams Museum, Deadwood, SD)

BUOYANT, wistful, little trail beaten hard by the booted feet of placer miners ran its crooked way to the first rich diggings in Deadwood Gulch. Close-built log cabins faced each other from behind pathetically important square false fronts across a rough road in the building of a Main street never intended for permanence. Ten thousand venturesome, excited gold seekers panned gold in the streams and crowded into the cabins in spite of orders from the United States Government to stay out of the Sioux reservation, and thus the outlaw camp of Deadwood was born. On the west, Forest Hill rose high and heavily timbered. On the east, White Rocks lifted their glittering limestone peak far above the noisy disorder of the young camp. Against every horizon mountains stood high and dark, in serene tolerance of the tumult at their feet.

The Government had recognized Deadwood's right to live and dig for gold by the time I set my sturdy little shoes on the board sidewalks of Sherman street to go to school in what was called "an old store building." I could not have been more than five years old. So, in a manner of speaking, Deadwood and I grew up together through stagecoach and school days until the railroad came in and I cried my way east to boarding school.

Of all the mining camps of the frontier, Deadwood flared highest and brightest. In one year it wrote a noisy, bloody page of history that traveled all over the world in a Wild West stagecoach and between the covers of dime novels. It was young longer than any town that ever grew and prospered because it was off the railroad longer.

For nearly fifteen years it was a stagecoach town and then one cold December morning the railroad came and in that one day the merry young mining camp bloomed into a surprised town with civic and moral obligations. It took it a long time to adjust itself and the twentieth century dawned to find it still youthful and still a little puzzled about its responsibilities.

Buffalo Bill, when he came into Deadwood on a railroad train for the first time, told me he was not surprised at the changes he found because railroads always aged a town. "A town is young," he said, "just as long as it stays off the railroad."

"It's too bad the railroad came," I commented.

"Oh, no," he said quietly but decidedly, "a town is like a baby. It either grows up or dies." And then he added with the ready optimism of the real Westerner, "But Deadwood, you know, was young so long it never will quite forget its youth."

There still is a wicked little fling to the very name. It carries a thrill of adventure even after all these years. A charmed something hung over the bright clean young fortunes that were made overnight with no capital but a pick, a shovel, and a gold pan. It flung itself into the days when gold was uncovered in wide, deep veins of ore, and stamp mills roared through the gulches. There never was but one Deadwood.

Law and order came early in '77 and for more than a dozen years lawlessness and law, order and disorder drifted along together in the seclusion of the deep, narrow gulch without interfering seriously with each other. They emphasized the natural sharp contrasts of the camp in Deadwood Gulch.

Everything was in dramatic contrast except material prosperity. There were no destitute poor. The richest among us had made their money in mines and that was something everybody else expected to do tomorrow. Or their rich ore veins might fault or pinch out any day. Wealth dug out of gold mines created no class distinctions. In everything else the contrasts were sharp and clear. Days were divided into high noons and sudden nights. There were no golden pink dawns and no purple twilights. Winter mornings were dark until the high sun leaped, fully day-blown, from behind White Rocks, and then it was nearly noon. Sometimes it found clouds floating around in its way below White Rocks and put them summarily to rout.

Somewhere in the middle of the afternoon before any sunset colors had time to assemble themselves, it dropped behind the pines on Forest Hill and day was gone. The seasons came in with a bang, and there you were. Only autumn slipped in gently at the end of a summer of bright days and crisp, cool nights and an occasional flurry of snow, trailing its purple veils over the gorgeousness of scarlet sumach, golden aspen, and scrub oak.

Deadwood was a wide-open town in the 'eighties with saloons and gambling houses and painted ladies—its spectacular vices on parade for all the world to see. But the homes on Forest Hill's one-sided streets and in the secluded hollow of Ingleside were as sheltered as the courtyard of a convent. What growing up in Deadwood saw of the other side of life merely was a it of highly colored drama that we didn't understand. We lived our lives in our homes, in school, Sunday school, church, and among the pines rocks, and wild flowers on the mountain that rose high above the houselines of the town, shutting us in, together with the "badlands," away from the rest of the world—so far away.

The lovely light ladies—pretty, beautifully gowned, and demure mannered—were, many of them, known by face and name to everybody. But their little span of glory was too brief to leave any illusion in our minds about the desireability of such lives. They collected their wages of sin under our very eyes. We saw them on the street, in the stores, at the theater on the rare occasions when there was a play at Nye's Opera House or Keimer Hall. And then, two or three years later, we saw those same girls pallid and shabby, with dingy old "fascinators" over their heads, slipping furtively down the alley that ran back of Main street, in quest of the price of a drink or a shot of dope. In a pathetically little while they disappeared. Once in a long time one of them married and escaped this fate. Some of them avoided it by the routine of poison or the little gun. Without anyone calling our attention to it, we accepted the drab skulking profession as the inevitable end of the easiest way.

Along in that dim alley parade went "Swill Barrel Jimmy," in his long frock coat turning all the sad apologetic shades of purple and blue and green when it should have been black. His trousers were frayed and fringy around his ankles. His derby matched his coat in color, and his hair hung in long messy strings over the clean white collar he always wore. He lived on the extravagant wastefulness of the Chinese restaurants, saloons, and houses of low morals and high charity. He slept where he could. On cold nights he availed himself of the cordial, unquestioning hospitality of the well-warmed saloons. He never was known to speak to anyone except the clerks from whom he bought his white collars and he made these purchases with as few words as possible. His gratitude to the saloon men who gave him shelter was expressed in a courteous monosyllable. No one knew of a certainty anything about him, but it was said that he came from a good old Southern family, had been an officer in the Confederate army, and at the close of the Civil War had wandered heartbroken into the West.

Everything about those alleyways was of deep interest. They were the arteries of a strange, different life. I knew very well that what we saw was the least of the difference. There was one elderly grande dame in Deadwood in those days, probably in her fifties, seeming older to us because old age was something of which the children of Deadwood knew nothing. It was something they never saw. For the town was young and its men and women were young. Only youth could hazard the hard journey across the plains from the railroads to the Hills. Only youth could make itself part of the town that Deadwood was in the 'eighties. This woman whose hair was beginning to turn gray and who had not danced since she donned her long, heavy, black veil when her husband died years before, was so venerable and so much the aristocrat that she could do as she pleased and go where she liked. The use she made of her privileges made me regret my own sheltered youth, for she made friends with the ladies of the badlands. She visited with them in their parlors where they raised the curtains just a little to let in a bit of afternoon sun in her honor. She never intimated in manner or conversation that she recognized any difference between their way of life and her own. She said she found them gay and companionable. They would laugh and talk together for a little while just as though she were calling on a new mining man's wife and then she would make her *adieux* politely and go home. But three times during the years she lived in Deadwood, girls whom she knew in this way came to her house on Ingleside and asked her to help them get away into something different. She did this as blithely and casually as she had paid her visits. I heard her tell my mother once, sitting in our quiet front parlor with its square piano, its books and pictures and warm, red carpet, that of course that was the reason she had gone and the three girls had more than repaid her for any trouble—if it had been a trouble which she said it all had not.

There was Nelly, she said, who always was rather a pitiful little figure, never quite adapted to the life. She was in Belle Haskell's house. Belle had been very kind in helping. She said some girls never could make good prostitutes.

Just then they discovered me sitting obscurely in my little rocking-chair intently reading Longfellow's poems, and Mother told me to go out and find Robbie and Gaylord. She hadn't heard their voices for some time and she didn't want them to wander too far from home. I obeyed very sadly and slowly.

I herded my little brothers home and then walked down the street to meet Father and the General coming home to dinner. They might have something interesting to tell and make me forget my disappointment over the unfinished story of Nelly.

Two men never were more unlike than my father and my mother's brother—the General—who made his home with us. Father was over six feet tall with black hair and mustache, dignified, and a little stern of aspect. General Dawson was a sandy blond with a long beard and his hat set rakishly at an angle. They came into the Hills a year apart, each in his own characteristic time. Father arrived in the spring of '77 after the treaty with the Sioux had been ratified. He came with an appointment from the President as Federal Judge with jurisdiction over all the Hills country.

He brought his family in the earliest 'eighties when the long stagecoach trail from the railroad was safe, and the little town in the gulch was comfortable. My own memory of the ride is that it was a delightful adventure. I think my mother disagreed with me. A stagecoach was a tireless thing. From the time it started on its journey, it never stopped until the end except to change horses and let us eat a little if we could get it. It rattled and rumbled and lurched all night as well as all day and you slept between the times you bumped your head against the side of the coach or fell off the seat. The water along the way was so bad that we carried with us bottles of cold tea—a most uninteresting drink. The most thrilling event of the night was the arrival at the stage station and the changing of horses. As we approached, the driver sent forth a clear, loud, "Yip-yip-yip, yi-yi-yi," to awaken the stock tender who had the fresh horses harnessed and waiting. We could hear their voices outside and through the narrow openings around the canvas curtains of the coach, we could see the lanterns and the shadows and dark bulks of the men and horses. Then the driver climbed to his high seat and everything was quiet except for the beat of the sixteen hoofs, and the dull thud of chunks of gumbo falling from the wheels. Sometimes it rolled up faster than it fell and then the driver, the messenger, and all the men passengers got down and scraped it off with spades carried for the purpose. Once when we were going into the Hills, the roads were so bad that we were delayed for days and we came to one dinner station where supplies had been delayed still longer and there was no food at all but beans—no bread, tea, coffee, or even salt. The wife of that stock tender was very unhappy about offering us such fare—utterly unadorned beans. But Mother, wise in the ways of traveling with little children, was carrying a lunch, and she shared her bread and salt with the stock tender's wife. When we came to places where they had dried-apple pie, we feasted regally. Once in the dark of the night we forded the Cheyenne River. The horses made a terrific commotion getting down the bank, and then the water splashed against us until we thought the whole river was coming in through the canvas flaps in a mad fury. Again, on the way, we met some men going out who had two small mountain lion cubs in a wooden crate.

Sometimes we saw deer and small herds of antelope. On one occasion, I remember, we saw a lovely purple mass against the horizon that looked like turreted castles in a beautiful mountain range, and Father said it was a mirage. Two days later I called his attention again to a ragged purple mass against the sky. "Another mirage," I exclaimed excitedly. He smiled and shook his head. "No, not exactly," he said. "Those are the Black Hills."

The General came to the Hills with the outlaws of '76. That wild young year and the Civil War through which he rose to the rank of general, were the highlights in his life. To Father the war had been an unpleasant bloody incident, his service an accepted duty. He had been far more interested in the peaceful building of a state.

The General's stories of those days of '76 were of unfailing interest, especially that of the centennial Fourth of July celebration. Here was a little band of outlaws on ground that belonged to wards of the nation, flying the flag, firing salutes, and singing national airs with enthusiastic patriotism. It was the General who read the Declaration of Independence and it was he who drafted the memorial to Congress that was read and signed that day petitioning that "honorable body for speedy and prompt action in extinguishing the Indian title to, and opening for settlement the country we are now occupying and improving." Further it earnestly requested "that the government, for which we have offered our lives, at once extend a protecting arm and take us under its care."

It is a tribute to the General that, in spite of the fact that during the year '76 he held the anomalous position of revenue collector, collecting government taxes from people who were not recognized citizens and who resented the injustice, he still was one of the most popular men in camp.

Late in the winter following that Fourth of July petition, the prayer was granted and the Black Hills were officially opened to white men. Four years later all the saucy little camps running down Whitewood Gulch and sprawling up toward Gold Run were gathered together into the incorporated town of Deadwood. We called them by their original names for a long time—Cleveland, South Deadwood, Ingleside, Elizabethtown, Chinatown, Fountain City, and Montana City. Deadwood itself never had been planned nor named. Early prospectors called the gulch in which they found their richest placer diggings Deadwood Gulch because of the burned timber on the mountain side above. They still talked about going "up to Deadwood Gulch," when the name included a cluster of cabins. As the camp became important enough to have a name, they gradually dropped the word "gulch" and the camp was thereafter Deadwood.

Forest Hill, sloping steeply up from the gulch on the west, was the only residence district included in the original Deadwood. The pines had been cut only where it was necessary for the building of the homes above their terraced dooryards on the three one-sided streets and at night the lamplights twinkled among the trees like friendly little stars. Williams street had been terraced out of the mountain and was the first as you went uphill. With no beginning and no end, it still was Forest Hill's one straight horizontal roadway. It appeared suddenly up on the hill above the flour mill in front of Henrico Livingstone's cabin, but it didn't begin there. It had come along obscurely from somewhere else. Henrico lived alone in a shabby little cabin and protected with a Winchester a mining claim she worked herself just back of the cabin. Sometimes she got into trouble with her gun. She had an unpleasant habit of throwing stones at the school children who strayed out of the school yard that backed up from Main street. I suppose she thought we wanted to jump her claim. The boys entered gayly into the stone throwing with the result that Miss Livingstone occasionally stalked, a tall grim figure, shabby, stiff, and dour, into the school room to lay her grievances before the principal. He always promised her courtesy and consideration, and ordered us to stay away from her. No one seemed ever to take into account that it always was Henrico who started the trouble. When I once called my father's attention to this, he said that he never had heard of her coming into the school yard to throw stones, and we had no business on her property nor any occasion to walk along the street in front of it. The surest way to keep out of trouble, he said, was not to run into it.

After leaving Henrico's warlike domain, Williams street swept its skirts clean between the Catholic and Baptist churches and by the time it came to the back fence of the school, was entirely fit for association with children. It was an excellent natural toboggan slide down to the corral and the bridge over City Creek after which it came into a confusion of corners where a lot of streets got off, with some difficulty, on their various ways.

The double line of houses that followed the little thread of a stream up a gently ascending gulch had a nice name of some sort that no one ever remembered. We called it "City Crick." On one side of the road the houses were reached by long flights of ascending stairs. On the other, short flights went down to the front doors. So far as I know City Crick went on forever. In all the long wanderings of my childhood, I never came to the end of it, nor passed the last house. Away up, somewhere, a man named Tilley had a cabin, a cross dog, a mild little boy, and a claim on the public highway. Sometimes he shot at people who tried to cross his property but nothing serious ever came of it.

Centennial avenue, starting at that same corner, was a long diagonal trail that twisted and curved up past the residences on its high side until it came, after all sorts of queer detours, to the shoulder of the mountain where there was an isolated house and garden. On the way up it passed a little old log cabin where the door always was closed and padlocked. Some one told me that a prospector lived there, that he was away all day prospecting and that he had thousands of dollars in gold dust hidden behind the locked door. I never was able to verify this, and I doubted it, even then. We used to stop on our way to and from long climbs in the woods to rest on his doorstep and gather sheep sorrel. Mother said she could make a salad of it if we got enough, but in spite of our valiant efforts we never did. It grew only in that one place. I tried hard because I had a lively curiosity as to what a sheep-sorrel salad would be like.

The only salads we knew anything about were of leaf lettuce, cabbage, and very rarely cucumbers, that we bought from a Chinaman who had a truck garden away down the gulch somewhere and peddled them around town in a little cart drawn by one horse. We made up for the sorrel deficiency by bringing in quantities of choke cherries, little gray-blue Oregon grapes that grew close to the ground, sarvis berries, and small red raspberries for pies. Living two hundred miles from a railroad in a country where no one troubled to raise fruit, we were dependent on the little wild berries we could gather, and the buffalo berries and wild plums the ranchers brought in from the valleys in the fall. My mother considered the lack of apples and peaches and grapes a serious deprivation. It grieved her, too, that our knowledge of woods was so limited in comparison with her own.

"My poor children," she used to say. "They know only two kinds of trees—pines and the others, whatever they may be."

She did us some injustice in that for we did know spruce from pines and we had a speaking acquaintance with birch and quaking aspens. But that she should feel sorry for us! That was the amazing thing. She whose childhood had been spent on an Ohio farm! She who had grown up in an *old* country that could not possibly have had any sympathy with children! We felt an unvoiced pity for her. Never as a child had she been friends with pines or climbed steep mountain sides thick with kinnikinick to come up on a divide and look down on all the world—on tumbled masses of mountains and sometimes even on clouds. She was of those who, as Badger Clark says, "never can understand the way we have loved you, young, young land."

She would have preferred to live where she had a large elm-shaded yard for her children to play in and long stretches of tree-shaded streets and country roads along which she could drive with her horse and buggy, her children piled in around her. Deadwood's drives were so narrow there always was difficulty when two drivers met, and they extended, for general daily driving, from tollgate to tollgate. When that grew monotonous one got reckless and paid two tolls and drove "around the belt," the triangle drive up Deadwood Gulch through Poorman Gulch to Lead, and back down Gold Run to Deadwood. If you went anywhere else, it was a long day's journey.

Shine street started from that confused corner and went down town on a slant past the Methodist Church and the old Wentworth Hotel and became something of a street in its own right. Its name was supposed to have been given it by some one who came from the capital of Wyoming but didn't know how to spell it and was a little forgetful of the number of syllables.

Williams street managed a couple of blocks more in the conventional fashion of having houses on both sides. It passed Lee street, a wide three-flighted stairway that dropped into an alley at the bottom of the hill and then picked itself up and went along like a regular street, cornering all the banks and being very important until it bumped into the foot of Mount Moriah just where Sherman street began.

Guy street catapulted down from Centennial with houses and stairs on either side of a rough perpendicular incline that was used for tobogganing in the winter and for nothing at all in the summer except on rare occasions when some reckless driver persuaded a strong, amiable team up or down.

At this point Williams street dropped her houses from the gulch side. They would have tumbled in anyway. A sidewalk with a railing ran along the edge of the hill, and twice stairways came up inquiringly from the gulch. After a comparatively long level stretch, the street lifted itself abruptly to "Nigger Hill" where one of the two colored families in town lived. Mrs. Goodrich was a kindly, mammy-like soul, and her children went to school and slid down hill with us. There was "Sad" Goodrich who got his nickname from his mother who, because he was not a merry infant, called him "ma sad baby," and the name clung to him always. There was Laura who was about my age and a little dark tower of strength. I remember one night when we were all coasting down Nigger Hill in the dark and I went over the side and halfway down to the bottom. I landed in a snowdrift and couldn't disentangle myself and I couldn't get any helpful attention from anybody until I heard Laura's soft, velvety voice. "Miss Estelline?" she called and when I shouted at the top of my lungs she came and pulled me and my sled out and took us back to the beaten track with apparently no effort at all.

"Old man Goodrich" wasn't as desirable a neighbor as the rest of the family. Once he brought a scurrying shooting scrap up into the narrow passageway between us and the house next door. I never did know what it was all about but there was a good deal of shooting and screaming and my little sister, Halle, and I followed the General when he ran out to see what it was all about. He saw her and told her to go back, but she didn't, and he never saw me, so we went on and peered down into the dark area way, the other house being considerably lower than our terraces. Pretty soon the General came back and the Goodriches went home and that was all there was to that. Nobody was killed and nobody was arrested. It was just one of Deadwood's ordinary little shooting scraps, that was all. The only unusual thing about it was that it didn't belong in our front yard.

If the children of lower Forest Hill came through their winters with whole heads and limbs, it was because the snow on the side hill was soft and deep and we grew so accustomed to tumbling about with our sleds that we didn't mind it. It required the utmost skill to keep in the street because it was so narrow. Teams could not pass and to make traffic of a sort possible a house every now and then stepped back accommodatingly and left space for a "turnaround."

From the top of the Goodrich's hill, Williams street paused a moment and then meandered off downward to nowhere in particular. Out in that direction there was a beautiful flat gray rock shadowed by a clump of pine trees. It was one of the most charming places in the world to sit on a summer day and meditate. The sounds of the town came up muted and mellow. Very faintly from Lead, three miles away, came the muffled roar of the Homestake stamp mills. The view of the town was beautiful, from the Hildebrand garden directly below, with its gorgeous masses of hollyhocks, to the mountains that shut in the gulch on every horizon. Hildebrand was a French Canadian with an express wagon and a large family of nice little boys who played with my brothers, and nowhere in all Deadwood Gulch was there such a flower garden as his, secluded behind his drab stone house and visible only from the hill above.

Forest Hill's second residence terrace was Forest avenue. It was no avenue at all, not even a street. It was just a sidewalk with houses fronting on it. They were very smart houses and the dwellers in them were very smart people. During the hectic mining stock boom of '86, it was known as "Iron Hill Row," because everybody who lived up there owned stock in Iron Hill, the silver mine out at Carbonate Camp that was so rich it started a new boom and kept it going. It paid dividends and did everything a mine should but it was a bad influence on the rest of Carbonate. It made every unscratched little location think it was a mine too. It was responsible for a gay summer in Deadwood, however. There had not been so much money in circulation since the summer of '76. People gave large parties in their houses. McClintock built an Opera House over his livery barn with four boxes on each side of the stage and a repertoire company played to good business all summer.

Father said that brilliant bedazzling boom, the like of which had not been known since the original discovery of gold in Deadwood Gulch, was an illustration of the western passion for balance, justice, and contrast, because it followed the continuous blizzard that encircled the Hills the winter before when all the cattle on the open ranges died and all the cattlemen went broke.

Ingleside, which shared with Forest Hill the distinction of being the best resident district of Deadwood, was the less western of the two. It cuddled in the hollow of the mountains on the east side of the gulch and was farther away from the heart of the town by the bias length of Sherman street. Its houses were surrounded by little yards and gardens and its people could not look down each other's chimneys as we did on Forest Hill. Neither did they have our flashing glimpses of the mysterious life of the badlands. Mother thought that was an advantage to them but one that was offset somewhat by their daily walk up and down Sherman street, shabby, shiftless, and no better than it should be.

It was not until the streets of Deadwood were later outlined brilliantly with electric lights that I noticed how they lay in a perfect Y. It couldn't be seen in the first yellow lights, shining out casually here and there from saloons and stores and the windows of the houses. Main street running straight up the gulch was the stem. McGovern Hill, obtruding its huge dark bulk between Deadwood and Whitewood Gulches, cut the forks. Main street swerved and took its line of lights up Deadwood Creek, and Sherman street trundled along up Whitewood.

At the foot of McGovern Hill, crowded sideways against it, stood the Congregational Church, Deadwood's pioneer place of worship. It was a crude, simple building with uncertain turning stairs leading up to the door, and no effort at decoration, inside or out, but it had opened its doors in the summer of '77 and ever since its half-dozen unslumbering eyes had watched the gulch that stretched straight before it to the badlands, and its little basement assembly room had been an important social gathering place.

We lived on Williams street at the head of the Wall street stairs, in a story and a half frame house with a mansard roof, a square bay window, and a scrap of a porch reached by steps that started for the bay window and then changed their mind and turned and led to the front door. From our steps my little sister and brothers and

I, the safe haven of our home behind us, could look down through the narrow slit to Main street and beyond to the foot of the mountain that stepped into Red Creek. Wall street was a naughty little thoroughfare that divided the good and the bad in Deadwood. It was known as the "dead-line" below which the police never interfered after six o'clock at night, and at each end it ran into a house of the sort that did not exist above the dead-line. One of them, "the 400," huddled under the hill directly below us, its roof in plain view. When we climbed down the steep hillside after chokecherries or a lost ball, we could see the darkly curtained windows but we never could get a glimpse inside. The house at the other end perched perilously over the creek and when the big flood came, it went down with the current. This might have served to point a moral if it had not been that the schoolhouse and the Methodist Church went too, while the Gem Theater and a lot of saloons stood fast.

Once I was sent on some imperative errand in the early evening guarded by our big dog, Danger. I was perfectly safe for two reasons. Danger didn't allow anyone to walk on the same side of the street with me as far as he could see them, and all good women and little girls were a sacred trust to Deadwood. But coming back I came through Wall street and up the long flight of stairs that ended at our doorstep and in its steep ascent ran the whole gamut of human morals. Back of one of the proud buildings on the corner that turned a haughty shoulder to Wall street and pretended it belonged only to Main street, was a row of three little one-story, dingy, white houses. They were so small that each front had room for only a door and one window. The night that I came that way with Danger, one of the doors stood open. A kerosene lamp shone gayly through a red shade, and in its circle of light a girl lay, apparently asleep, on a couch. She had a pretty, delicate young face with long dark lashes lying against her cheek. Masses of wavy dark hair fell over her elaborate, lace-trimmed pink negligee. I stopped to look at her until Danger growled and I hurried on up the stairs. She was a picture I never forgot and for years did not understand, but for some reason that I could not have explained, I never spoke of her to anyone, not even to Irene, my chum, with whom I held long and frequent naive discussions concerning the badlands and their careless, mysterious inhabitants.

Home looked very cozy and dear and safe when I came in out of the dark. Mother was sitting in front of the fireplace with Mrs. Mather—pretty, gray-haired, gentle Mrs. Mather—and they were talking about the church supper next week. Mrs. Mather said Mrs. Hastie would make an angel cake and she was the "boss angel of this town." Mother was mending a pair of small trousers. She said she would make some lemon jelly and that Irene and I would wear French peasant costumes and wait on the table.

From the dining room came the light clink of silver and china. Our Norwegian maid, Alamena Marie, was setting the table. Mother told me to go out and tell her to put on an extra plate. Mrs. Mather was staying for dinner because Mr. Mather was out at the mine and wouldn't be home until late. I came back and sat down on a pile of floor pillows beside my mother. She paid no attention to me but that didn't matter. Her soft voice went on exchanging kindly gossip with Mrs. Mather and I wondered if the sleeping girl I had seen through the open door could have had a mother anything like her.

We saw a good deal of interest go by the little rift of Wall street. We used to watch the stagecoach come in with a proud flourish, and the long trains of patient bull teams with their covered freight wagons pull slowly up the street. We counted the wagons and oxen as they passed and made small wagers with each other as to their number. We were natural born gamblers all of us. We played poker for matches and whoever lost had to go to bed in the dark. We did that until Father stopped us because he said he didn't want the boys to learn to gamble. He didn't think Halle and I would carry it to the danger point. One summer later on, when Mother and the other three children were down at the Springs, I acquired the habit of going with Irene and Mose Lyon and Louis Caulfield out to the races every day. I bet on St. Patrick's Day because of his name and his beauty and I won a lot of money. I think it was four dollars. It was so much that I couldn't conceal the possession of it from my father and he put a stop to that too. But counting oxen and covered wagons was a slow, quiet amusement. The stagecoach arrival was different. That was the grand excitement of the day as long as we were a stagecoach town. Its six white horses came up the gulch on a gallop. The driver on his high seat flourished his long whip in skillful skyward sweeps, the dingy white canvas-covered coach lurched and rolled from side to side with its distinctive rumble and our one brief daily tangency with the far world beyond the mountains and across the plains swaggered to an abrupt stop in front of the Merchants Hotel. The stagecoach was the herald from the world that lay beyond the White Rocks and the tumbled mountains that rolled up around them. It brought a four-day-old Chicago paper, letters from strange places beyond the Missouri River, and passengers who as recently as last week had seen a locomotive and a train of cars. Sometimes it brought capitalists with money to develop mines. We could hear it coming while it still was a long way down the gulch and always we rushed to the window or the front steps, according to the weather, to watch its disjointed dash past Wall street—four horses at a time and then the other two and the coach. That's how narrow Wall street was. It was a wonderful experience to be on the wooden-canopied porch of the Merchants Hotel when the stagecoach arrived. I wanted to go down there every day and wait for it, but that wasn't my mother's idea of proper conduct for a little girl.

I was sure that Father and the General never told us everything that happened. For instance, there was the woman with her three children who came in to meet her husband only to find that he had shot himself that afternoon. I didn't know the man and I don't remember his name, but the General said he had lent him money two or three times during the winter because he said he was expecting his family that day on the coach. Father said he had given him money on several occasions for the same reason. He had borrowed it that way from nearly every man in town and never did the family come, until that day when nobody believed him and he could borrow no more. He was a gambler with poor luck and the day the family finally came he didn't have even the price of a meal. Father and the General couldn't make up their minds whether they were glad or sorry that he hadn't asked them that last day. They were afraid they might have refused like the others and been filled with regret. On the other hand, they might have given it to him and there would have been no tragedy. Mother thought it was too bad he hadn't seen one of them.

Then there was the time an old prospector from somewhere up around Ragged Top came down to meet a woman with whom he had corresponded through a matrimonial paper, and when he saw her, she was so homely he ran away. She identified him by his running and went after him, and he had to marry her anyway. I never heard how it turned out.

If the stage was on time, Deadwood's dinners were on the table by the time the mail was distributed and the men got home. If it were late, the whole schedule of our daily life was disordered. And sometimes it was several days late! It had a thousand good reasons for delays even though Indians had ceased troubling when the treaty was signed, and road agents, the masked highwaymen of the Hills, had abandoned their nefarious practices. More than nine hundred and ninety-nine of these reasons had to do with the heavy gumbo roads through the real Badlands—not Deadwood's moral badlands. Sometimes the Cheyenne River swelled and rose so that the ford was impassable for days. It was not an easy journey from Sidney or from Pierre. No wonder the horses, the stage, and the driver were proud and boastful when finally they reached Deadwood.

Below the badlands, Chinatown twisted along its narrow picturesque way, housing the largest Chinese population ever achieved by any town of the size of Deadwood, outside of China. In the shabby little shops were piled great quantities of beautiful Oriental silks, embroideries, egg-shell china, sandalwood, teak and carved ivory. There were innumerable laundry shops. The clothes of Deadwood were as thoroughly washed as the gravel in the creek. There were gambling games that no one interfered with—naturally, considering the number that ran wide open for the pleasure, profit, and occasional tragedy of the white man. A joss house painted brown with little red embellishments pointed and peaked and squared itself in unexpected ways and places. On the outside it was unlike anything else in all the Black Hills. The inside we were never permitted to see. A peculiar and intriguing odor of incense came to meet you a block away. Its religious hold on the Chinese was not universal, however, for many of them came to the Chinese school at the Congregational Church and one, expressing his new faith through his art, ornamented a wedding cake with raised pink sugar letters explaining that "God made the world but Wong made this cake."

My father was the unofficial counsel for the Chinese and the connection was valuable to us in many ways. Always in emergencies he could commandeer a cook or dishwasher on a moment's notice. When there was not a Chinese servant to be had in the whole gulch, one would spring up from some dark corner at Father's bidding and come cheerfully into our kitchen. They were real Chinese in those days too, wearing queues wound round their heads and loose, dull-blue trousers, and long shirts. At Christmas time and on both their New Year's Day and our own, dozens of Chinamen brought us rare and lovely gifts of an infinite variety from embroidered crepe shawls and Satsuma teapots, to scarlet chopsticks which we tried hard to use but were discouraged by the family, especially Mother, because of the amount of rice we spilled over the tablecloth.

Father's service to his Chinese clients consisted entirely in seeing that they were given fair trials when they were arrested for selling opium. I think he always managed an acquittal. Neither judicial nor public opinion was very strong about such things. If a Chinamen wanted to smoke opium, who cared? They rarely were in trouble about anything else. I remember once, in my later teens, I slipped into a night police court with Father because, as we were coming home from prayer meeting, a Chinese client stopped him, and he didn't know what else to do with me. A Chinaman had quarreled with a gambler by the name of "Little Gus," over a white woman, and Little Gus had emerged from the affair so much the worse for the Chinaman's bread knife, that his friends demanded speedy justice against the "chink." I never forgot Little Gus's face as he sat in that basement court room dimly lighted with a few inadequate kerosene lamps. The white bandage around his head intensified his pallor and his beautiful dark-lashed blue eyes as he lifted them to Judge Early on the bench were innocent as a baby's. He had the face of an angel but a record in the badlands that acquitted the Chinaman.

When Wing Tsue, the leading Chinese merchant, brought his wife from China, he announced to the white men of his acquaintance that she would be at home on their New Year's Day and he would be glad if the wives of his friends would call on her. They did. I went with my mother. We were ushered in through Wing Tsue's dim, fragrant store and up a steep outside stairway to the small ordinary looking house that clung to the hill and gave no evidence of the warm luxury within. The apartment in which our hostess received us was heavily curtained and draped, richly furnished in teak and enamel, and the air was thick with the odor of sandalwood and Chinese punk. Mrs. Wing Tsue herself was the loveliest bit of exquisite china I ever saw. She was painted and mascaraed in a way no nice American woman could understand in those days but on her the effect was charming. Her black hair was built in a high pyramid with gorgeous pins and combs. Her brilliant silk jacket and trousers were heavy with embroidery, and her tiny useless little feet were encased in embroidered satin shoes with wooden soles. She spoke no English but her gentle gracious manners and her courteous solicitude about the serving of tea and the delectable little almond cakes, small candied limes, and other bonbons made us feel as if we had talked over all the polite topics of the day with her.

She returned our calls a few weeks later, driving out in the finest carriage behind the highest-stepping team that could be commandeered from Job Lawrenson's livery barn, and Job Lawrenson, a pioneer, had the best horses and equipages in the Black Hills. I am sure it was the only time she ever left her rich, close rooms. But her children went to the public school and to Sunday school. She was the only "respectable" Chinese woman that ever came to Deadwood. Later she and her little girls went back to China and after a while Wing Tsue and the boy joined them. But that was a long while after.

The other Chinese women—the ones that Mrs. Wing Tsue did not know—lived in the "cribs" along that part of Main street that ran through Chinatown, and beckoned to passers-by. But they could not have belonged to the underworld for the term was not used in Deadwood. Everything was too open and aboveboard.

The gayest thing about the Chinese was their funerals. They marched up Main street and Sherman, and around up the steep Ingleside way that led to the cemetery on Mount Moriah, scattering little red pieces of paper with Chinese characters on them. They were intended to distract the attention of the devil away from the dead, some one told us, and we gathered them up with much interest. Always marching with the Chinese in their funeral processions was Dr. von Wedelstaedt, the one white man who belonged to the Chinese masons. He was a tall, straight, dignified Prussian, family physician to half of Deadwood, and carrying a personal interest not only in our health, for which he felt entirely responsible, but in our general welfare no less.

"Don't look so cross all the time," he used to tell me. "Be pleasant like your sister." And to Halle, "Why don't you stand up straight like your sister? You'll have to stand up straight or you can't marry my boy, Bismarck."

He had jet black hair and whiskers and when he marched with the Chinese he wore his high silk hat, swung his goldheaded cane, and threw his head and shoulders back, proud of being the only man of his race among the Chinese masons. But he never could learn to eat with chopsticks. When he went to eat bird's nest soup and dried ducks with his friends he carried a spoon in his pocket.

At the other end of Main street, the Indians who used to come from the Pine Ridge and Rosebud reservations to attend United States court pitched their tepees and received their guests. We were a very friendly people in Deadwood. We went to see everybody who came to town. On one of these visits a hospitable group of squaws insisted that I join their dance and we shuffled and hopped around the fire to the wailing music one of them made on a queer little instrument, and we were just as chummy and happy as though we spoke the same language and our forefathers had not believed that the West was too small for two races. We had come so far in the late nineteenth century as to believe that Deadwood Gulch was wide enough for as many races as could find it. My squaw friends couldn't speak any more English than Mrs. Wing Tsue could, but between the little Oriental in her dim, stuffy, scented rooms, and the Indian squaws in their wind-swept, fire-lit tepees with the stars shining in, there was a distance greater than the length of all the Main streets in America linked together. Between them came all the rest of us—miners, lawyers, stage drivers, merchants, gamblers, doctors, priests, saloon keepers; women with their memories of older, gentler lands, and children growing up with their minds and hearts full of the glory of the old mountains and the charm of the young camp; men from the farms and villages of the prairie states, and men from the "effete east," political exiles from Europe and remittance men from England, and men whose pasts could not travel by stage. We were all children of the present and the future. No one was ever curious in old Deadwood. No one ever asked a man "what his name was back in the states."

"MADAME MOUSTACHE AND POKER ALICE"
FROM *UPSTAIRS GIRLS: PROSTITUTION IN THE AMERICAN WEST*
MICHAEL RUTTER
2005

Frontier women made up a unique and engaging chapter in Deadwood's colorful history. While many assumed traditional roles in the household and in commerce, others were attracted to the seamy side, the backstreets, the brothels, and the bars. A distinct few became enchanted with the felt of the gaming tables, using their feminine wiles and an insider's knowledge of poker and faro to win miner's hard-earned gold dust.

Two of the most colorful women of the West were Madame Moustache and Poker Alice, both of whom became fixtures in Deadwood's early-day history and the legends of today. Prolific writer and researcher Michael Rutter opened a window on the story of prostitution in the American West with his 2005 book, Upstairs Girls. *Shining his light on the world's oldest and often most unattractive profession, Rutter's expose also captures the characters who sometimes succeeded in their initial pursuits, only to be diminished by a hard life of late nights, sordid companions, and strong liquor.*

Though Madame Moustache and Poker Alice worked many of the burgeoning towns of the West—the former in the Sierra Nevadas of California, the latter catering to soldiers of Fort Meade at Sturgis, South Dakota—they made their names in Deadwood, where a mere mention of their monikers still conjures up a picture of a fuzzy lipped madam and a cigar-chomping poker aficionado. Here then are the stories of Madame Moustache and Poker Alice, followed by Rutter's sometimes humorous list of "creative professional names" used by prostitutes in the Old West.

Madame Moustache: The Gambling Madam

She's the best woman gambler in the West.

—Poker Alice discussing Madame Moustache

A pretty nineteen-year-old French girl named Simone Jules decided to leave home and head to California—to seek her fortune in the gold fields. Simone concluded that there was wealth to be mined, not from the ground but from the miner's pockets; faro was her game of choice. If that didn't work, she would find another way to get her share of the pie.

It's unclear if Simone was from France or if she was a Creole from the Mississippi Delta country. To the men of the Gold Rush, it didn't matter. Any French woman was a luxury and she carried a premium price—to look upon, to gamble with, or to rent for the evening. In the West, French girls held a strange fascination—something Simone was aware of and capitalized upon.

In San Francisco, she took a job at the Bella Union working the gambling tables (among other things). She was ambitious and didn't intend to work for someone else for long. She wanted a business of her own. Simone surely was successful and made enough money to realize her dream.

By 1853 Simone had saved enough to purchase her own business. She changed her name to Eleanor Dumont and opened up the Dumont Gambling Palace and brothel in Nevada City, California, about 140 miles east of San Francisco. She wanted to be closer to the mines and the men who worked them. Legend has it that on her grand opening there were free drinks for everyone—champagne flowed like spring water. Her gambling house was a big success as she rode the gold boom. Mining towns were a bit crude for her taste, but she liked the action and the gold dust. She didn't like swearing and discouraged gentlemen from cursing in her presence. Eleanor, the gambling mistress, madam—and occasional prostitute—was at the top of her game. She had one of the hottest places around.

While at the Dumont Gambling Palace, she decided to take on a junior partner—the man who happened to be her lover at the time.

For a while, their live-in business arrangement worked. Her prince made a fine wage, treated her like a queen, and got a small percentage of the action. It wasn't long, however, before their personal and business relationships began to sour. She knew a gold digger when she saw one. Eleanor got fed up and gave her man his walking papers. She still loved him, but she wasn't going to give up all she'd worked for, as well as her independence, for a man.

Legend has it that she wasn't much of a drinker until this time. After counting her money and staring at her lonely room, Eleanor consoled herself in 90-proof comfort. She took refuge in what appeared to be her only true love, a deck of cards.

By 1859, the boom was starting to die out. Eleanor sold the Dumont Gambling Palace and moved on—which proved to be her pattern for the rest of her life. Eleanor would go to a mining town when the strike was hot, work the tables and the carnal desires of the miners, usually as a madam, and move on before the town went bust.

She left the Sierra Nevadas and headed to the promising fields of Bannack, Montana, where she ran another gambling house and a brothel. While she was in Bannack, dark fuzz became noticeable on her upper lip. It grew more and more prominent. Eleanor was still a pretty woman and attractive to men. However, one night a hardrock miner got a bit too drunk and impolitely called her Madame Moustache. Even though it was whiskey talk, the moniker caught on. For the rest of her life, this was her handle. Over the years Madame Moustache worked most of the gold and silver towns in the West— hoping the cards would turn for her.

She had a reputation as someone not to mess with. In Colorado's Hoffman House, she whipped a man she caught cheating at cards. She was formidable with a crop, a bullwhip, and a handgun—having killed several men in her life for various reasons.

She and Blonde Marie ran rival houses of ill repute in Tombstone, Arizona. They were bitter competitors. The two had a few shouting matches, but managed to keep their differences to the red light district. Madame Moustache's business was located on Sixth Street, and although she ran a smaller house than Blonde Marie, Madame Moustache was quite successful; her house was always busy. Certainly part of her success could be attributed to her advertising efforts. She'd doll all her girls up in their finest clothes, hire an expensive carriage, and run up and down the streets promoting her establishment.

While she was in Deadwood, South Dakota, she was reported to have been friends with Calamity Jane, and it was thought that Madame Moustache taught her the finer points of poker. Considering what an unsuccessful gambler Calamity was, Madame Moustache was either a poor teacher or it just wasn't Jane's game.

In her travels across the West, Madame Moustache had accumulated quite a sum and was known as an astute gambler. Men came from far and wide to match cards with her. In approximately 1870 she cashed in her considerable holdings and bought a ranch near Carson, Nevada—she wanted a place to call home and semi-retire. The good madam sought a quiet spot away from the buzz of the gambling halls and the demands of managing houses of prostitution: sore losers, temperamental painted ladies, and randy cowboys. A ranch was considered a good investment and she wanted to watch the grass grow.

Madame Moustache was eager to settle down and embrace the joys of domestic life. She'd found love and married. Marital bliss was fleeting. Around 1872, her new groom absconded with all her life's savings, causing her to lose her ranch. All she had left were her clothes and a few jewels—personal items her gold-digging husband managed to overlook. While the cavalier groom took all she owned, he never got a chance to enjoy his ill-gotten gain. Madame Moustache caught up to the rake and opened him up with a double blast from a 12-bore shotgun. She was never charged with the crime, although she was suspected. She denied that she was responsible, but said she wasn't sorry he was dead. The question of his death would have remained a mystery had she not confessed to shooting him shortly before she died. She never got any of her money back.

Instead of a quiet retirement, after her husband's death she found herself back on the gambling-whorehouse circuit, going from mining camp to mining camp. She was bitter and fatigued. Both her looks and gambling skills began to slip. She was drinking more and making desperate attempts, emotional attempts to win—something a professional gambler doesn't do.

Indeed her lifestyle had once been quite grand. She had known financial success and adventure, and had rubbed elbows with some of the great characters of the West, from places such as the California Gold Rush mining towns, Deadwood, and Tombstone. She knew Big Nose Kate, the Earp Brothers, Doc Holliday, and other gunfighters.

After an illustrious career, the woman known as Simone Jules, Eleanor Dumont, and Madame Moustache finally lost the last of her money at the tables. In Bodie, California, on September 6, 1879, she went home and pounded down a few drinks to get numb. Then she poured a healthy slug of champagne, topped it off with prussic (or hydrocyanic) acid, and drank it down.

The Sacramento Union reported that "a woman named Eleanor Dumont was found dead today . . . having committed suicide." According to the *Black Hills Daily Times,* "She took her chances in that great undiscovered country."

Poker Alice: A Gambler, a Madam, a Bootlegger

They say I drink whiskey, my money's my own
And they who don't like me can leave me alone
I'll eat when I'm hungry, drink when I'm dry
I'll do what I please and live 'til I die

Jack of Diamonds, Jack of Diamonds, I know you of old
You've robbed my old pockets of silver and gold
O whiskey you villain, you've been my downfall
You've punched me and kicked me, but you'll have it all.
Verses from Jack of Diamonds,
Late Nineteenth-Century Western Folk Song

She lived for games of chance. Many times she bet it all on the turn of a card. Poker Alice was a gambler with steel nerves and a winning smile. She loved to play cards, chug down tumbler after tumbler of whiskey, and smoke cigars.

Poker Alice was born Alice Ivers on February 17, 1853, in Devonshire, England, many historians believe. Some argue she was born in Sudbury, England, in 1851; others wonder if Alice was actually born in Virginia to Irish immigrant parents.

The Ivers family went to Colorado when Alice was a teenager. Her father was employed in Leadville, Colorado, as a schoolteacher. The pretty young Alice turned the heads of the local boys, but she fell for a mining engineer named Frank Duffield.

The marriage seemed to be happy, but the fates had other things in store for this young woman. One day, Duffield miscalculated when he was setting off a charge of TNT in the shaft and was killed in the subsequent explosion.

Before his untimely death, Frank had taught Alice the finer points of card playing—especially poker. The young bride was a quick study, as the young couple played cards into the night. Thanks to her husband, she had hopelessly fallen in love with poker (among other games of chance). Blushing bride Alice had a feel for the game, too. Before long, she was much better than Frank, who was supposed to be a pretty fair hand. Once she became a widow, Alice, not one to worry about social conventions where cards were concerned, took a bold step: she endeavored to become a professional gambler—not exactly a widely accepted career at the time.

While she was well educated for her day, Alice couldn't see herself teaching school or sewing shirts for pennies an hour. Poker and faro had a much bigger thrill and a much bigger pay off; and she wanted to make playing more than just a hobby. She found the risk-taking exciting. Plus, it was fun to take men's money—and a lot easier than laboring away in a traditional job. Alice took what money she had and started hanging out in gambling halls.

POKER (ALICE) (DEALING) (TUBBS)

FERO BANK GAME DAYS '76

Poker Alice Tubbs was notorious on the felt, operated a brothel, and became a Black Hills legend. (Photo courtesy of the Adams Museum, Deadwood, SD)

At the time, this was rather unacceptable behavior for a "decent" woman. Folks must have talked about what the schoolteacher's daughter was doing—playing cards like a painted lady in saloons, and with her husband barely cold in his grave. Alice wasn't without scruples. She refused to work or gamble on Sunday. She needed a day of rest.

Her first efforts produced big results. She won a number of good pots and smiled at her good luck. Alice had made more in a few evenings than her father made all year teaching school. Rumor has it she pocketed her winnings and made a quick trip to New York on the steam car to buy a new wardrobe. She knew she was a good-looking woman, and some fancy clothes would spruce up her image as a professional. Widow Alice was aware that men liked to gamble with a pretty girl. It's said she lowered her neckline to keep the men she played with interested—and distracted by her ample cleavage.

Alice gambled as she moved from boomtown to boomtown. At one establishment, she is reported to have broken the house. At this time she started to pick up the habit of smoking rather large cigars when she played. She also developed another life-long habit: guzzling hard liquor.

In 1890, she was in Creede, Colorado, a new mining town, hoping her luck would hold out. She worked at Bob Ford's gambling house managing gambling tables. She did well for herself, garnering quite a reputation as a skilled but honest card player. Several years later, Alice left Colorado and headed to Deadwood, South Dakota.

While she was dealing poker in Deadwood, she met an enthusiastic gambler named Warren G. Tubbs. His day job was painting houses in Sturgis (he was a better painter than a card player). Over the tables, the two got acquainted and eventually a romance developed; they soon married. The newly wedded lovebirds bought, of all things, a nearby chicken ranch and they raised a family. It was a happy match for the two. Neither gave up their true passion: gambling. Alice would supplement her egg money with her poker winnings. A careful woman, she carried a .38-caliber pistol when she gambled. They raised their children in the process, Alice sliding off to make a few bucks and getting out of the house for an evening or two a week. Alice states that the couple tried their best to keep their kids away from gambling and saloons.

They lived together happily for some time. Warren became ill and was diagnosed with tuberculosis. Alice gave up gambling while she took care of her husband. They moved onto the plains near Moreau River, where the air was drier, making it easier for Warren. Finally, in the winter of 1910, Warren died. Alice placed the body in a buckboard and drove him back to Sturgis for burial. She then went back to work doing what she knew best, playing poker. No longer a pretty young woman, she still drew challengers who wanted to take on the famous Poker Alice (it's unclear when or why she earned the nickname).

Still a skilled player, she built up her savings and opened an establishment of her own between Fort Meade and Sturgis on Bear Butte Creek. With Warren gone and her children grown, Poker Alice decided it was time to expand her horizons a bit—adding the title Madam Alice to her professional vita. Soon, she got a loan and expanded her house. She also went on a trip to round up girls for her petite poker palace/brothel. Some have written she went off to Kansas City to get her girls, but that seems a long distance when Deadwood and Denver were a lot closer. With Fort Meade nearby, her house was in a good location to attract soldiers looking for some diversion—girls, gambling, and liquor.

It was also at this time that she found love again in the form of George Huckert. George was another gambler with whom Alice had become acquainted. Some say he had loaned her $1,000 to invest in her house and that she married him so she wouldn't have to pay it back. It didn't really matter since poor George died shortly after they were married.

During the following summer, Alice's business ventures thrived. The army held maneuvers in the region, and there were several conventions that brought in love-starved men. Business also increased the summer of 1913 when the National Guard was training nearby.

If Poker Alice's legend can be believed, her popular little house of ill repute was a bit over-booked one evening. A number of the soldiers were on leave and had converged on her place. Alice locked the doors until things settled down. The men outside weren't happy about this and started to raise a ruckus. It's likely they had more than a few drinks. Before long, the situation escalated, and they cut the phone and electric wires going into her establishment. To make matters worse, the soldiers started throwing rocks through the windows. Alice wasn't one to take matters lying down—she'd had enough. The no-nonsense madam fired a few warning rounds through the window. As bad luck would have it, she hit two of the men from the South

Dakota National Guard. One man is supposed to have died in the hospital, the other recovered from his wounds.

The police were soon at Alice's door and took her and her soiled doves to jail. Apparently, the good judge was one of Alice's clients and he looked upon her with some favor. Alice was able to dodge the shooting charges—since she wasn't firing at anyone in particular. She and her girls were charged with prostitution, and Alice was charged with running a disorderly house. Alice paid the fines, and she was back in business.

By this time, Alice was long way from being a spring chicken and had put on a fair amount of weight. Excessive drinking and the constant string of cigars were starting to take their toll on her health. She'd long ceased worrying about how she looked. For years she'd taken to wearing a beat-up old hat, a large men's shirt, and a khaki skirt.

Her business wasn't as lively as it used to be, but she was still getting by. Prohibition added new life to her ventures. Soldiers from Fort Meade could get a drink at her establishment and maybe play a game of poker. She was busted several times for bootlegging. In 1928 the Governor of South Dakota pardoned Poker Alice, who was seventy-eight and in failing health, on the charge of bootlegging. Governor Bulow said he didn't want to send a white-haired lady to prison.

In poor health, Alice hoped gall bladder surgery would help her ailments; she did not recover. She was buried in Sturgis, South Dakota, in the Aloysius Cemetery. Tourists can still visit her gaming house, which was moved to Junction Avenue in Sturgis.

CREATIVE PROFESSIONAL NAMES

Annie Fanny	English Gussie	Nervous Jessie
Beautiful Doll	Fatty McDuff	Nervous Nellie
Belle Bird	Fighting Annie	Nosey Kate
Big Bonanza	Foozy	One-Eye Evelyn
Big Butt Annie	French Irma	Oregon Mare
Big Dollie	Frenchy	Peek-a-boo
Big Em	Fuzzy Girl	Peg Leg
Big Hattie	Galloping Cow	Peg Leg Alice
Big Minnie	Grizzly Bear	Peg-Leg Annie
Big Mouth Annie	Gumboat Sue	Poker Alice
Big Nose Betty	Hambone Jane	Queen
Big Nose Kate	High Step Jennie	Queenie
Black Hills Bettie	Irish	Raunchy Rachael
Black Hills Kate	Irish Meg	Red Light Lady
Buffalo Joe	Irish Queen	Roaring Gimlet
Bulldog	Jew Annie	Rockin' Chair Emma
Calamity Jane	Jew Jess	Rowdy Kate
Careless Ida	Kitty Kirl	Sadie the Calico
Chicago Joe	Klondike Kate	Sadie Sow
Cock-eyed Liz	Lady Jane Gray	Sallie Purple
Connie the Cowboy	Lady Luck	Santa Fe Moll
Contrary Mary	Lattice Porch	She Wolf
Cotton Tail	Lazy Lil	Sizzlin' Kate
Crazy Horse Lil	Lazy Liz	Sloppy Sue
Crazy Horse Lillie	Light Lil	Smooth Bore
Cuttin' Lil	Little Gertie	Spanish Liz
Diamond Lil	Little Gold Dollar	Spanish Queen
Dirty Emma	Little Lost Chicken	Squirrel Tooth Alice
Dirty Mouth	Lost Chicken	Sweet Annie
Dutch Annie	Mexican Maria	Tit Bit
Dutch Jake	Mollie May	Venus Whore
Dutch Kate	Molly d'Damn	Whory Dory
Dutch Katie	Mustang Me	Wicked Alice
Dutch Mary	Nellie the Pig	

"LIKE ONE FORSAKEN"
FROM DIARY ENTRY
W. E. ADAMS
1925

Three days, three deaths, one family. W. E. Adams was one of Deadwood's most successful merchants, a man who built his legacy in the town's most turbulent times. His home, now preserved as the Adams House Museum, was among the most opulent in the West, with carriage houses, maid calls, leaded glass, intricate friezes, imported Italian marble sinks, and Persian rugs. His gift to the city—the Adams Museum—still stands as one of the Black Hills' premier venues for the exploration and interpretation of early life on the Western frontier.

When gold fever struck the Black Hills in 1876, W. E. went prospecting, and his brother, James, bought a restaurant in the uncharted region. But, when James opened the Banner Grocery Store later that summer, W. E. joined him as a partner. When James moved to California in 1889, W. E. bought out his interest, expanded the business into wholesale grocery activities, and became wildly successful.

Adams was a man who seemingly had it all, until a series of events unraveled his world. The resolute businessman had already lost one daughter to typhoid fever in 1912 when, in the course of just three days, June 6–8, 1925, he lost his wife, Alice M. Adams, his daughter, Helen May Adams Benton, and his granddaughter. After burying all of them, Adams sat down and wrote, forlornly, in the family Bible, the following.

Deadwood, So. Dakota Nov. 15, 1925

W. E. Adams, who married Alice May Burnham December 22, 1880 had hoped we both would live to celebrate our fiftieth anniversary

W. E. Adams, who bequeathed the Adams Museum to the town of Deadwood, is shown here, circa 1925, about the time he married Mary Mastervich. (Photo courtesy of the Adams Museum, Deadwood, SD)

and now, after forty-five years of married life find myself deprived of my loving wife and both of my dear daughters.

I feel like one forsaken and do not see ahead of me in this world much if any happiness. I do hope I shall have the physical & moral strength to follow the teachings of my dear mother who passed from this Earth in 1877 in Minneapolis, Minn., and when I join my wife and daughter in the great unknown I hope none may say with truth I did not keep the faith for their memory is very dear to me.

PART IV

THE LEGEND CONTINUES

———————

While many of America's frontier towns simply faded into the prairies, coulees, and forests from which they arose, Deadwood has stood the test of time. In a series of booms and busts, the community has striven to stay relevant, and to maintain, preserve, and interpret its cultural and historical resources.

Google "Deadwood" today and you'll get nearly 6 million "hits," or more than 4,000 for every one of its 1,380 residents. With the following excerpts, we explore an original television series tied to the town's colorful past, Deadwood's place in modern country music, the haunted spaces in this mountainous place, and the use of Deadwood as a backdrop for historical fiction.

"The Color: Gold Makes a Man a Man and Lifts Us Up Above the Baboons" from *Deadwood: Stories of the Black Hills*
David Milch/Home Box Office
2006

When famed producer David Milch brought HBO's original series
Deadwood *to America's television screens in March 2004, no one had
ever seen anything quite like it. Villains fed their victims to the pigs
and sophisticated intrigue rivaled that of any Machiavellian tale.
Drill-dusty miners, saloon-keepers, whores, card sharps, and even the
occasional respectable character, of which there were relatively few,
swore up a mean streak with equal abandon. Web sites tracked cuss
words by the quarter-hour, while historians debated whether inhabitants of the Wild West really spoke like that. When the dust settled
three seasons later,* Deadwood *had been branded as one of the most
critically acclaimed dramas on television, earning two Emmy Awards
and a Peabody along with a Golden Globe for actor Ian McShane.*

*The real-life town of Deadwood, on which the series was based,
reveled in it all, hosted half the cast of the show twice, and watched
its visitation soar. Today, nearly two million annual visitors flock to
the gold-filled gulch to stop by the infamous Saloon No. 10 and stand
beside the graves of Western legends such as Wild Bill Hickok and
Calamity Jane, both of whom found their permanent residence in
Deadwood's own Boot Hill—Mount Moriah Cemetery.*

*But, long before there was television, Web searches, and lei-
sure travel, there was gold. In the following excerpt found in a
book spawned by the success of the HBO series, Milch* (NYPD Blue,
Hill Street Blues) *explains the lure of gold and all it could buy in
Deadwood's earliest days.*

Deadwood is an animal town, driven by sex and greed and violence. At the center of Deadwood is the nineteenth century's most mind-bending symbol of value: gold. They're all after it: Swearengen, Farnum, Tolliver, Joanie Stubbs, Hearst, and the grizzled prospectors and placer miners who spend their money on drinks at the Number Ten Saloon. Gold drives the camp's economy, and it serves to organize the experience of being on the frontier, where the uncultivated landscape would otherwise seem meaningless.

But the trick of gold in Deadwood is that as soon as a man has it, its quality weighs on him: What's a yellow rock worth, really? That's when he swaps it for girls and booze, and relieves himself of the misery of mental life.

All the distinctive forms of human civilization begin in the mud, with the activities of prospecting, drinking, gambling, whoring, and fighting that you see in a gold rush town like Deadwood.

The initial transaction of gold for drink or gold for sex gives rise to a more complex social order that is traced in the development of Deadwood. Everyone in town takes up a position in the social order that is based on the premise that gold has value. Al Swearengen says, "While I agree with you that gold is worth twenty dollars an ounce, my gift is not for prospecting, because I don't like water freezing my nuts. But I will bring you women, and to the extent that we agree on the value of the gold, then a woman sucking your cock or doing one or another thing is worth gold in the amount of X, Y, or Z." And that's how the town of Deadwood is born.

The agreement to believe in a common symbol of value is really a society trying to find a way to organize itself in some way other than, say, hunting or killing. I read somewhere that baboons cannot move in groups of more than forty because they have to be able to see the leader. Humans need to see only the totem of the leader. If you can symbolize the leader, you can begin to organize in larger groups. You are no longer confined to tribes. We can fly the Stars and Stripes, or hold up a cross, and those abstract symbols are more powerful to us than the person of any president or pope.

Timothy Oliphant as Seth Bullock, right, and Keith Carradine as Wild Bill Hickok, left, prepare to draw in the critically acclaimed HBO original series *Deadwood*. In real life, Bullock was a successful businessman and close friend of President Theodore Roosevelt, helped manage the country's first national forest, and founded the present-day town of Belle Fourche. (Photo courtesy Home Box Office, Inc.)

Agreeing on this single symbol of value has allowed us to organize our individual energies on a wider scale. If we've got to barter wheat for barley and barley for shoelaces, everybody is going to fight. "I worked seven months on these shoelaces and you're going to give me one sheaf of wheat!"

I wanted originally to do a show about Rome, because that was the point where the organizing principle of humanity moved from pure force to in hoc signo vinces, "In this sign we conquer." And when I wound up in Deadwood, I just changed the organizing principle from the cross to gold. Deadwood was the last of the great gold strikes, other than in Alaska, where it is frankly too cold to set a dramatic television series that would focus on anything else besides the extremity of that climate, with long haunting shots of the ice and the wind-driven snow.

The gold rush is a phenomenon that is unique to the English peoples. The great gold rushes in history take place in the wider sphere of English settlement—in North America, in South Africa, and so on. Gold was discovered in Siberia, for example, but there was never a Trans-Siberian gold rush, or an Ottoman Turkish gold rush, or a Spanish Jesuit gold rush. In my mind, this has something to do with the explosive tension between the promise of equal legal and political rights in English society and the reality of a class-bound society in which men are not equal.

Deadwood, like other gold rush towns, was a kind of reenactment of the founding of our country. When gold was discovered, there was a rush toward a new territory, followed by a collective regression from society—thus, the Wild West. And later, there was a regeneration of society seemingly de novo, from new. That happens in the hopes the contradictions of the old social order will finally be resolved. But once the news comes of a strike, settlement patterns immediately change.

Waves of prospectors and parasites, merchants, fortune hunters, displaced persons, and government bureaucrats rush in to this new space, bringing with them all the old forms of civilization from which the first wave of adventurers had fled.

The bank panics of 1873, just before the discovery of gold in the Black Hills, were the result of complicated manipulations and distortions of money produced by people who understood there were realities at the level of the symbol that you could fuck with. Namely currency, which is the symbol of value brought to a new level of abstraction: an amount of silver or gold that represents a greater quantity of silver or gold, or a piece of paper represents a portion of a gold reserve that is said to exist in a vault somewhere. It was estimated in 1875 that two-thirds of the currency in America was counterfeit. The thing that the symbol was supposed to represent, gold, occupied a very tenuous position in regards to the object you held in your hand, which was probably fake. A gold strike offers a way to get back to the supposed reality of the symbol—to find real gold. This is much the same way a gold strike promises a social space where the promise that all men are created equal will finally be fulfilled, and every man-jack among them will be a king, outside the falsifying structures of social classes and legality.

But one of the appeals of gold is the idea that there's no connection or respect for the land, cycle of seasons, and so on. You go in and rape the land. It's a source of pleasure, as one would imagine. One of the reasons you can't hold onto the gold, as it turns out, is because it's merely a source of pleasure. It doesn't produce anything; it doesn't ground you. So it attracts a particular personality and then brings out the worst in him.

When times are tough in a place where there's a connection to the land, there's a hope that things will get better. When a gold camp starts to go bad, people are gone like Ricochet Rabbit and on to the next place. There's no respect for the place. It doesn't generate any obligation or debt. You don't want to be in that kind of place in the end.

If you're out there in pursuit of gold, what is the real physical behavior that you're engaged in? You're freezing your balls off in a stream. You're telling yourself, "This gold is a source of power." But in fact, it's just a fucking rock in a stream. In the grip of that disjunction you very quickly feel the need to be in an environment that participates in the symbol's importance. So you can say, "This gold buys me booze, women, drugs, gambling, a sense of my own importance."

The only reason the town of Deadwood exists is gold. Why do men and women hold gold as an object of value? There is no purpose to gold. Gold doesn't do anything except serve as a repository of emotion. Something in us that is specifically human has the capacity to endow a symbol with a special meaning. The fact that the women, the pimps, the drug dealers, and the saloonkeepers agree with the prospectors upon the value of the symbol and begin to organize their behavior in acknowledgment of the worth of the symbol confirms and furthers the power of that symbol in the minds of every hoople-head, placer miner, saloonkeeper, and whore in Deadwood and beyond.

Swearengen has recourse to some ideas of stability and right conduct to help protect his business and to keep from wasting too much of his energy, since he can't solve every problem himself. He also has accompanying needs for human connection and sympathy, as dubious as these may seem to the purely rational part of his brain, that arise from the fact that Al is human. These needs, of the businessman and the human being, create complicating swirls and eddies of the civilization that the citizens of Deadwood were attempting to escape.

Meanwhile, the presence of gold brings in all these new people from the outside: hardware stores selling tools to the miners and telegraph wires to keep markets informed of the quantities of gold that are mined, which influence the market price of gold in London and Zurich.

And hardware store owners and telegraph operators have their own needs, which in turn must be served by more outsiders. That's why the world of Deadwood keeps getting more complicated, as alliances are formed and discarded, and new realities evolve that have their own influence on the situation, which is always fluid and evolving. That's how the civilizing game is played.

This process hardly reaches its limit in Deadwood. Once a symbol separates from reality, there is no real limit on the amount of power that can be unleashed. Einstein's ability to conceive of the universe in an equation, in a symbol, $E=mc^2$, liberated the fundamental energy of the universe.

Einstein never visits Deadwood. It's not that kind of show. But there is George Hearst, who is the monstrous abstraction of the symbol made flesh. Hearst understood what gold made possible. The only price he had to pay was to treat human beings as if they were inanimate. That's a version of original sin. But original sin got us out of the garden and got us to Manhattan.

Hearst was an obsessive, focused only on one thing. I read a fragment of an autobiography he wrote, and he just couldn't stop his numbers from populating his brain. He would try to have a different idea, he would write about the Yellow Peril or something, and then he would lapse back into his numbers, "Then I bought this and we combined it with that." It's one of the horrible manifestations of human possibility, and particularly of the path that we have now taken, which is irreversible—namely, the universal organization of mankind around the symbol of gold.

"Deadwood Mountain"
from *Horse of a Different Color*
Big Kenny, John Rich, Paul Worley
2004

Before successful country western music stars Big & Rich ever recorded a note together, they traveled from Nashville to the heart of America's Outback—the Black Hills—to write in seclusion and raise a little hell.

    *Deadwood's enduring legends and lore, and a colorful cast of characters past and present, became the impetus for many of the songs on their first platinum Warner Bros. Records' album—*Horse of a Different Color. *In addition to the smash hit, "Save a Horse, Ride a Cowboy," among the songs on the debut album was "Deadwood Mountain." Since its release, Big & Rich have returned to Deadwood numerous times to use the community as a backdrop for music videos and a one-hour Country Music Television special* Big & Rich: Alive in Deadwood. *Most recently, Big Kenny has become a major investor in one of the town's mega-projects—The Deadwood Mountain Grand Hotel & Resort.*

DEADWOOD MOUNTAIN
I've been a rambler, all my life
Been a bet it all gambler
Yeah I let it all ride
Never been afraid of losin'
Yeah there's been times I've lost it all
But it won't really matter
Someday when I'm gone

You can bury me on Deadwood Mountain
By my brother Wild Bill and sister Calamity Jane

In the first decade of the twenty-first century, Deadwood became the adopted home of the smash country duo Big & Rich, perched here high above downtown. Big Kenny and John Rich spent weeks in the historic town writing many of the songs for their debut Warner Bros. Records album, *Horse of a Different Color.* (Photo by Johnny Sundby, courtesy of Deadwood Chamber)

Don't bring me no flowers
Just a six gun smokin'
Put me eight feet down
When you bury me
Put me eight feet down
When you bury me

When your heart runs deeper
Then a ghost town gold mine
You just know your bound to find that mother lode
You'll spend your last heartbeat chasing after rainbows
No there's no place you won't go
To win one more time

You can bury me on Deadwood Mountain
By my brother Wild Bill and sister Calamity Jane
Don't bring me no flowers
Just a six gun smokin'
Put me eight feet down
When you bury me
Put me eight feet down
When you bury me

And cover me a little extra deep
Cause that's the only way
I'm ever gonna rest in peace

You can bury me on Deadwood Mountain
By my brother Wild Bill and sister Calamity Jane
Don't bring me no flowers
Just a six gun smokin'
Put me eight feet down
When you bury me
Put me eight feet down
When you bury me

"Haunted Spots"
from *The South Dakota Road Guide to Haunted Locations*
Chad Lewis and Terry Fisk
2006

Armed with a quirky mission and a funky format, Unexplained Research *investigators Chad Lewis and Terry Fisk explored the shady history and enduring mysteries that remain in the Black Hills in their 2006 work,* The South Dakota Road Guide to Haunted Locations. *In particular, the pair's account of a foray into Deadwood's ghostly past is remarkable for its breadth, as well as its entertaining presentation.*

From the untimely death of Wild Bill Hickok before his fortieth birthday to the ghost of lawman Seth Bullock, who still haunts his namesake hotel on Deadwood's Main Street, the account takes readers on a romping journey past strange modern-day occurrences, unusual smells, moving furniture, and phantom apparitions that have even caused guests to check out in the middle of the night.

The Bullock Hotel

Location: Deadwood, Lawrence County, South Dakota
Official Name: The Bullock Hotel & Casino
Address: 633 Main Street, Deadwood 57732-1123
Phone: (605) 578-1745
Fax: (605) 578-1382

Ghost Lore

A lot of travelers like to visit the various historic sites and buildings of a town. Usually, every town has at least one or two historic places hidden in them; unless, of course, that town is Deadwood.

You see, Deadwood does not just have one or two historic sites; the whole town is listed as a historic landmark. Deadwood's history is overflowing with unique characters and one of the most famous is Seth Bullock. In addition to being a hardware store owner and hotel proprietor, Bullock was Deadwood's first Sheriff.

As Sheriff, Bullock looked to bring some much needed order to the renegade town. Bullock was known far and wide as an imposing man with an ice cold stare that even gained the respect of Deadwood's most unsavory characters. Those who knew him believed that he could outstare an angry cobra or a rogue elephant. If you are looking to stare down his grave, you can find it high up the hill in Mt. Moriah Cemetery. Yet if you don't want to hike to the top of the hill to stare at his grave, then you can check into his haunted Historic Bullock Hotel where you may have a chance to stare him down face-to-face.

- The hotel is haunted by the former owner who refuses to leave.
- The *Unsolved Mysteries* television program featured the hotel on one of their programs.
- Strange apparitions still linger throughout the hotel.
- Several of the rooms are said to be very haunted and guests have captured proof.
- Phantom footsteps have been heard walking throughout the hotel.

History

1884—Seth Bullock met then-US Deputy Sheriff Theodore Roosevelt. The two became good friends.

1890s—Roosevelt appointed Bullock to the position of first Forest Supervisor of the Black Hills.

1894—After a fire destroyed most of the Deadwood Hardware Store, Seth Bullock bought the land. Bullock, a former hardware store owner, was the first sheriff in Deadwood. Seth had a mission to bring order to the outlaw town.

1895—Seth constructed the Bullock Hotel. The three-story

Deadwood lawman and entrepreneur Seth Bullock built the Bullock Hotel on Main Street in 1895 as a symbol of the town's emerging prosperity. It's said that his ghost still haunts the place. (Photo courtesy of Deadwood Chamber)

sixty-room hotel cost nearly forty-thousand dollars and took nearly two years to complete.

1896—The hotel was completed and opened to an excited audience.

1900—Bullock acquired a small building on the south end of the hotel. This addition is currently part of the hotel.

1905—President Roosevelt appointed Bullock to the position of United States Marshall for the District of South Dakota.

1910—President William Howard Taft reappointed Bullock to his position.

1913—President Woodrow Wilson also reappointed Bullock to his position.

1919—President Roosevelt passed away.

1919—Bullock erected a monument to honor Roosevelt on Sheep Mountain.

1919—Seth died of cancer in room 211 of the Bullock Hotel. His body was buried in the Mt. Moriah Cemetery along with other famous Deadwood citizens Calamity Jane and Wild Bill Hickok.

1976—Many original items from the hotel were auctioned off when the Aryes Family sold the building.

1990s—The Historic Bullock Properties Group bought up several historical buildings in Deadwood. The goal of the group was to restore the buildings to their original splendor.

During renovation, the Bullock Hotel converted the over sixty rooms into twenty-eight rooms in order to make the rooms larger and more spacious.

Investigation

The hotel was featured on *Unsolved Mysteries*. The ghosts of the Bullock Hotel were showcased during a 1992 episode.

Guests staying in rooms 205, 207, 209, 211, 302, 305, and 314 have all reported paranormal activity.

In the basement of the hotel sits Seth's Cellar Restaurant. The restaurant staff informed us that while they were working throughout the restaurant, they would hear the piano mysteriously play an old ragtime tune on its own. They believed that the ghosts of the hotel were upset that the restaurant had been moved.

Plates, glasses, and barstools from Seth's Cellar Restaurant are often seen being moved by some phantom force. We spoke with one patron who was amongst five other people who all witnessed a glass flying off the rack from above the bar and crashing on the floor. The bartender casually quipped that the ghost does this all the time. Many people believe that Seth's Cellar Restaurant is the most haunted location in the building.

Guests and staff report that the barstools in Bully's Bar will be moved by some unseen force. Even more bizarre are the reports that the chairs next to the bar's fireplace will often re-arrange themselves.

Several staff reported that they will be working throughout the hotel when they spot a ghost of a tall imposing man walking through the halls. Often times the ghost will disappear into thin air or will simply walk through a solid wall.

Several guests have reported that while relaxing in the hotel, they heard a ghostly male voice call out their name. Most were extremely baffled when they found no one else was around. Other guests report being tapped on the shoulder by unseen hands.

Staff informed us that many visitors request room 211 while staying at the hotel. Room 211 is the room in which Seth died. Those brave enough to spend the night in room 211 report seeing the ghostly apparition of Seth.

A guest told us that they were staying in the hotel for a vacation. They left the hotel for a while to go explore the historic town. Upon returning to the room, they were shocked to find that someone or something had moved all of their possessions around.

Often guests spending the night in one of the haunted rooms report that the room lights will turn off and on by themselves.

We spoke with several maintenance staff who informed us that many times while working in the hotel, they would leave their cleaning carts directly outside of a room, but when they return the carts will have been moved. Although this phenomenon takes place quite often, staff have still not found a cause.

Both staff and guests have reported hearing the eerie sounds of phantom footsteps in the hallways of the hotel. Those brave enough to peek out of their rooms never seem to find the cause of these ghostly footsteps.

One man was staying at the hotel and had no idea of the haunting activity that has made the hotel famous. He was extremely puzzled when he saw the ghost of a tall man walking the hallway near his room. The guest reported that the ghost just disappeared right before his eyes. After seeing a photo of Seth Bullock, the man was convinced that the ghost he had seen near his room was Seth.

Seth's ghost is actually quite a popular ghost, as it is one of the most frequently seen ghosts of the hotel. Many of the witnesses report coming face-to-face with the unmistakable ice cold stare that made Seth so feared and respected while he was alive.

The ghost of Seth Bullock also seems to appear when employees are taking a break or appear to be working at a slow pace. Many believe that even from the grave, Seth is trying to keep a watchful eye on his employees.

A couple and their seven-year-old grandchild were staying in room 306. The young child left the room in search of the vending machine. The child got twisted around and soon became lost. The grandfather was starting to get worried when he opened the door to go search for the child. Much to his surprise the child was standing right outside the door. The child explained that he had gotten lost and that someone had helped him find his way back to the room. The next day, while checking out of the hotel, the young boy pointed to a picture of Seth Bullock and exclaimed "Look, that's the nice man that helped me find my way back to the room!"

Seth's ghost is not the only spirit seen in the hotel, as others have reported seeing the apparition of a young girl in the hotel. The girl is seen mostly in the basement where young children were kept during the typhoid fever and small pox outbreak in Deadwood.

Visitors to the casino often report catching the strong scent of roses and lilacs while on the casino floor. These mysterious smells often take place during the winter months when the natural smells of the flowers would be less likely. These smells are believed to be from the perfume of the lady ghost that roams the first and second floors.

Other ghostly smells of the hotel include a roaming cigar odor that lingers in places that no one has been in or smoked in.

Several perplexed guests have reported hearing the sounds of a woman weeping along with sounds of a crying child. However, much to their amazement, when they look out into the hallway no one is there and the eerie noises stop.

A cowboy staying at the hotel during the Days of '76 event was partaking in an afternoon nap when someone kept knocking at his door. Upset at the loss of his nap, the cowboy waited at the door for the perpetrator to strike again. When the knock came again, he opened his door and could see another cowboy standing out in the hallway. He flung open the door to catch the prankster, but was mystified when the cowboy he had just seen was not there. The man reported that someone then shoved him into the hallway and slammed the door behind him.

The radios in the hotel are often changed from a modern station to a country music station. This phenomenon is even reported when the radios are unplugged.

A woman staying in room 313 approached the front desk with her alarm clock. She reported that she had unplugged it because the light of the clock was keeping her awake. At approximately 2:30 am, the alarm clock went off by blasting country music. The woman was so spooked that she refused to allow the alarm back into her room.

Another guest of room 313 showed up at the front desk in her pajamas. This woman had awoken from her sleep to find a man in a cowboy hat standing at the foot of her bed. She was so shaken by the encounter that staff had to pack up her belongings because she refused to return to the room.

THE GREEN DOOR

Location: Deadwood, Lawrence County, South Dakota
Official Name: Wild West Winners Casino
Address: 622 Main Street, Deadwood 57732-1111
Phone: (605) 578-1100
Toll-free: (888) 880-3835

Ghost Lore

At one time Deadwood was famous for its brothels that operated openly, albeit illegally. Every year, during deer hunting season, the train would pull into town with scores of men who had convinced their wives they were on hunting trips, but were in fact after a prey of a different sort.

Although the houses of prostitution have long since been shut down, many believe the "ladies of the night" still haunt the night in the back rooms and dark corners of what used to be one of Deadwood's most popular brothels—the Green Door.

During a cold winter in the 1920s, a prostitute gave birth and hid the baby from the madam for fear of losing her job. One night a customer discovered the crying baby in the closet and killed it in front of the horrified mother. Today people can hear the ghostly infant crying upstairs.

Another version of the story is that a young prostitute was severely beaten by a customer and left to die in a closet. The ghostly sounds of her sobs can be heard coming from the closet. Other stories follow a similar vein . . .

- People close the closet door, but find it has mysteriously reopened on its own.

- Hushed voices, laughter, and footsteps are heard inside empty rooms.

- Other doors upstairs will open and close on their own, but most often, they will violently slam shut.

- Eyewitnesses have seen objects move.

- People experience the feeling of being watched or that somebody is standing behind them when nobody is there.

- Phantom "ladies of the evening" have been seen peering from the upstairs windows.

- Objects mysteriously move or are misplaced from the bar downstairs.

History

1897—The original building was constructed for the Salvation Army. It was later destroyed by fire.

1903–1906—The building that currently stands was constructed and used as a brothel.

1950s–1980—Hazel "Dixie" Fletcher operated the Green Door brothel in Deadwood.

1980—Federal law enforcement agents shut down the Green Door. Other brothels that were raided included the Purple Door, the Beige Door, and the White Door.

Investigation

The original building that was the Green Door is now a part of the Wild West Winners Casino. Employees report that most of the haunting activity occurs in the upstairs which is not open to the public and, unlike the rest of the building, has never been renovated. It looks just as it did when it served as a brothel in the early 1900s.

Employees report their uneasiness about these rooms from the past and confirm the reports of the mysterious slamming of the doors and other ghostly activity. Management discourages the employees from going upstairs, but one Halloween some of the workers secretly went up there and afterwards would only say that the frightening things they encountered were enough to convince them the place was haunted.

The second-story windows overlooking the street do have mannequins of the turn-of-the-century ladies of the evening. It is not certain if people have mistaken these for apparitions or if the sightings had occurred long before the mannequins were ever there.

It should be noted that although Saloon #10, where Wild Bill Hickok was killed, no longer stands, the Wild West Winners Casino is built on the original location. The original saloon was destroyed in a fire and relocated across the street.

MISS KITTY'S

Location: Deadwood, Lawrence County, South Dakota
Official Name: Miss Kitty's Casino
Address: 649 Main Street, Deadwood 57732-1123
Phone: (605) 578-7778
Toll-free: (800) 873-1876

Ghost Lore

Many of us complain about our jobs and dream of being in a different line of work, but could you imagine being trapped in an unwanted job even after death?

Claire was a former slave who worked as a cook at Miss Kitty's in Deadwood. What she really wanted to do was to be an artist. In her spare time, when she could afford the materials, the talented young Black woman would brush paint onto canvases and create beautiful portraits, still lifes, and landscapes—artwork that nobody would see or appreciate.

Ultimately, her unfulfilled life ended tragically when she was murdered. After her death, she was quickly forgotten, but her frustrations with work and aspirations to be an artist lived on.

Most of the haunting activity centers around the Schnitzelz Restaurant in Miss Kitty's.

- An artist's paint brushes have materialized in the basement and various places in the building.
- A customer felt bristles brushing against her arm, looked down, and found a sable brush. Moments earlier nothing had been there.
- One employee felt her hair being touched and played with by unseen hands.
- Items would be mysteriously misplaced. Things would be lost and reappear the next day in another location. It's common for things to be mysteriously moved from the upstairs to the basement or vice-a-versa.
- Plates, silverware, and glasses will be moved or rearranged.
- One employee, fed up with the mischievous pranks of the ghost, challenged Claire to show herself. At that moment a plate flew across the room and shattered against the wall. After that, no more challenges were issued.

History

Little is known about the history of the building, except that it was built around the 1900s and may have been a restaurant in the past.

The Schnitzelz Restaurant (now changed) is a recent addition to Miss Kitty's Casino. The Schnitzelz chain was started in Canada by German immigrant Jack Niemann and features a unique German menu.

Investigation

Because the haunting activity was becoming more frequent, the staff decided to call in a psychic. It was the psychic who identified the ghost as Claire and determined that it was the presence of the restaurant that disturbed her.

Another center of spiritual activity is the basement under Miss Kitty's. This is the original cellar with a rock foundation and dirt floors. Most of the employees are too creeped out to even venture down there. It is not known why so much ghostly energy is concentrated in that spot. We could speculate that if Claire was a laborer in a kitchen, then food and supplies may have been stored in the basement, making it necessary for her to make frequent trips down there. Others speculate that perhaps this was where she was murdered. For all we know, she could even be buried under the dirt floor.

Historical investigations have not turned up any records to verify the historicity of Claire, but our research is ongoing.

MOUNT MORIAH CEMETERY

Location: Deadwood, Lawrence County, South Dakota
Phone: (605) 578-2600
Directions: From US 85 (Sherman St) in Deadwood, turn (east) on Cemetery St. (becomes Van Buren St) turn left on Lincoln Ave. (becomes Jackson St), enter cemetery parking lot.

Ghost Lore

Mount Moriah is without doubt the most famous cemetery in South Dakota, and many would even say it's the most haunted. Strange things have been reported here.

- A sense of being watched and followed while strolling through the cemetery.
- Feelings of unexplained fear and trepidation.
- Apparitions of phantoms wandering in the Chinese section.
- Moving shadows late at night.

History

1877 or 1878—The Ingleside Cemetery was started in an area in Deadwood known as Whitewood Gulch. According to the Deadwood Cemetery Association, Rufus Wilsey was the first buried here. The *Black Hills Daily Times* maintains that it was James DeLong.

1878–1880—About 350 infants and children died from an outbreak of diphtheria and scarlet fever and were buried in the cemetery.

1879—As Deadwood rapidly grew, level ground became prime real estate for homes and businesses, so the town decided to move the cemetery to the top of a hill and rename it Mount Moriah cemetery. Because the grave markers were made of wood, many of them had deteriorated due to time and the weather, consequently, not all of the graves were found and relocated. Occasionally, even to this day, bones and skeletons will be unearthed in the Ingleside area.

1938—The Deadwood Cemetery Association turned the cemetery over to the city for lack of funds.

1999–2002—The city of Deadwood spent $3.5 million on a cemetery restoration project that refurbished monuments, rebuilt walls, restored ironwork and masonry work. They repaired the streets, installed curbs, and paved roads. Landscaping work was done and a visitor center was constructed.

Investigation

Every year between 80,000 and 100,000 people visit the cemetery.

Records exist for 3,627 burials. Many of these people died from natural disasters such as floods and fires, some died from accidents, and others were victims of murder. Other causes of death listed by the Deadwood Cemetery Association included: Childbirth, "bad whiskey" (a euphemism for alcoholism), opium, catarrh, dropsy of the heart, summer complaint, softening of the brain, inflammation of the bowels, want of vitality, "God knows," killed by Indians, teething, old age, hobnail liver (cirrhosis), broken thumb, struck with bar glass, hanged by vigilantes, and from eating 14 hard-boiled eggs.

Many of the Chinese who worked in the mines had guarantees written in their labor contracts that within 10 years after their death their bones would be disinterred and shipped back to China. They believed that if they were not properly buried on Chinese soil, their ghosts would eternally wander the earth. Unfortunately, many of the remains were not exhumed, and they remained buried in unmarked graves at Mount Moriah. Some visitors to the cemetery claim to have seen the spirits of these Chinese workers wandering through the graveyard late at night, unable to find eternal rest.

We spoke with two young employees of the cemetery who told us of their bizarre encounters while working there. The girls stated that while preparing to close the cemetery, they often would walk through to make sure no one was left inside. While strolling past gravestones the girls would often catch a glimpse of a shadowy figure roaming the cemetery. However, the employees could never track this figure down.

We spoke with one employee who was convinced of the cemetery ghosts. She reported that during the evening while walking through the cemetery closing the gates, she would turn around to find that someone or something had mysteriously reopened the very same gates she had just closed.

Employees told us that while closing up in the gift shop, they would often hear strange noises coming from the cemetery. Upon listening closer, they would hear what sounded like mysterious voices engaged in conversation within the cemetery. Concerned that visitors might still be in the cemetery they would go to investigate, yet every time they went to check it out, they found the cemetery completely empty.

So much paranormal activity has taken place at the cemetery that several employees told us that they did not want to work alone due to fear.

"WE'RE ALL OUT OF TOUCH"
FROM *DEADWOOD: A NOVEL*
PETE DEXTER
1986

Raw and unfiltered, Pete Dexter's Deadwood: A Novel *brought a Western town to life in ways that made the reader variously squirm, smirk, and roar. In dialogue as clear as an unmined creek, Dexter stages a Wild West fueled by the lure of gold, the simplicity of sex, and the suddenness of violence in what the* Washington Post Book World *claimed "may well be the best western ever written." Devilish, delightful, and detailed, the 1986 work from the author of* Paris Trout *and* Train *explores the human condition, pointing out every weakness and frailty, exalting in every human kindness.*

In the following excerpt, an unvarnished account of the arrival of two friends—Wild Bill Hickok and Colorado Charley Utter—to Deadwood in the summer of 1876, Dexter greets a wide-open place of mud, blood, and beer, random gunshots, whiskey by the barrel, and Mexicans carrying human heads on Main Street.

Bill and Charley had been in Deadwood four hours when the Mex rode into town carrying the head of an Indian. He held it up, away from the giant pieces of slop that were coming off his horse's hoofs, yelling some kind of Mexican yell. He rode to the bottom of the badlands, and then back up into the respectable part of town, and then back into the badlands. It was the most excitement since the wagon train, and the miners and roughs followed him up and down the street—some of them making the same noise that he was.

"What is it?" Bill said. He and Charley were standing at the tent across the creek from their wagon, trying some of the fifty-cent whiskey. The man who owned the tent had given them the first drinks free. He said it was an honor to own the spot where Wild Bill Hickok first set his feet on Deadwood soil. He said he might put up a sign to commemorate it.

"It looks like a Mexican on a stolen horse carrying somebody's head," Charley said.

"That's an Indian," said the man who owned the tent. He'd hung calico on the inside walls to brighten the mood. "There's a town reward, two hundred and fifty dollars for any Indian, dead or alive."

"That one's dead," Charley said. His humor sometimes grew an edge when he drank.

Bill shook his head. "I never heard anything like that. Paying Mexicans two hundred and fifty dollars to kill Indians."

The man who owned the tent poured them another shot. There had been twenty or thirty others there drinking with them, but they'd left now to follow the Mex. "It's the law," the man said. "It used to be twenty-five dollars, but it went up after what they done to Custer."

"Custer?" Bill said.

"Kilt him and everybody with him. Two, three hundred boys of the Seventh Cavalry up to the Little Big Horn in Montana." Bill shook his head. "June twenty-fifth," the man said. "You didn't hear that?"

"We been out of touch," Bill said.

"We're all out of touch," the man said. "The pony express—shit, you might as well just walk out here and deliver your messages in person. But Custer's a fact. Terrible mutilations, no survivors." He waited to build the suspense before he told Wild Bill what kind of mutilations, which had been the focus of conversation in town ever since the news arrived. "A polite way to put it," he said, "if Custer had survived, he wouldn't of had no eyes to see, and he'd of had to squat to piss."

As soon as the man said that he saw it hadn't set right with Bill. Maybe they were friends. He tried to soften it. "That being the case," he said, "he's better off dead."

Bill finished the shot and headed off in the direction of the Mex. "I didn't mean nothing," the man said to Charley. "I was just explainin' the problem."

The Prince of Pistoleers poses for a studio portrait in all his Eastern finery. Cautious and controlled, James Butler Hickok fought in the Union Army, then traveled West as a stagecoach driver, before serving stints as a scout, lawman, and professional gambler. He died in Deadwood on August 2, 1876.

(Photo courtesy of the Adams Museum, Deadwood, SD)

Charley watched Bill walk across the street, his chin up, not even looking at the mud, and then down the other side into the badlands. They were shooting guns down there now, and Charley wondered where the boy was. Lord, don't let the boy get shot. Charley Utter had lived thirty-seven years, most of it unworried and natural. He'd hunted and fished and run trap lines into all the tributaries of the Grand River. When they'd found gold in Colorado, he'd bought and sold claims. When the gold began to peter out, he ran supplies into the newer, more remote camps. He'd made more money than any miner he knew and held on to most of it. He'd been shot twice in the legs by accident, hunting, but he'd never had to pull a gun on a living soul. As much as you can, he'd even gotten married on purpose.

It did not sit with him that now, in the space of a spring, he was dreaming at night of Bill's blindness, and doing everything for the boy but powdering his ass. It wasn't that they'd asked him, it was like a sickness he'd caught.

Two different sicknesses. He'd been to the edge of the canyon with Bill, and could predict him better than anybody alive. He was tied to Bill, who was like his own person. There was one side that got Bill women and money and included the stories people told about him, and there was another side he kept to himself. Except Charley felt like he was keeping Bill's private side for him now. The public side was as wild as ever—a reputation always changed slower than a man—and more and more, Bill occupied himself in that. Charley imagined that it was the blood disease, or going blind, but Bill sometimes seemed to lose track of the line between the stories and what was true.

The boy, on the other hand, was a problem connected to his wife, and when Charley worried about the boy, it was the purest self-interest. Charley's wife was named Matilda Nash. He'd married her on September 30, 1866, when she was fifteen years old. She was the cleanest human being Charley ever saw. She had readable eyes and pale, English-type skin, and she used to sit on the bearskin rug he'd given her father with her chin pressed against his knees and believe every lie he told her about the places he had been and the things he had done.

Her father was a baker from Bath, England. Charley had a picture of that place in his head. Her mother had died at the birth of Malcolm. Everything considered, she did the honorable thing. Tilly brought the boy up herself, mad at him every minute, complaining about him to anybody who would listen. And she would kill you if you agreed with her.

And after the boy and her father were asleep, she'd sit at Charley's feet—he didn't sit on the floor himself because of the ache in his legs—and listen to his stories. She seemed to understand everything he said, including the way it was between him and Bill. It never occurred to him that she was sitting there smiling, making lists of things she was going to change.

Charley opened his pouch and watched the man who owned the tent pinch out enough gold dust to cover the cost of what they'd drunk. Whiskey was less than two dollars a gallon back in the States, and what the man took had bought maybe twice that. "The overhead doesn't hurt you much here, does it?" Charley said, looking around. He was always interested in how people made a living.

The man smiled and leaned closer. "I don't know nothing about that," he said, and Charley could see that was probably true. "You think I could still put up a sign?" he said. "I don't want to do nothin' to upset Wild Bill more than he is."

"He won't mind," Charley said, and started off.

The man said to tell Bill he was welcome to come by and look at the sign anytime he wanted. "And you too," he said.

Charley walked back down into the badlands and found Bill in the company of the Mex and Captain Jack at the bar of the Green Front Theater. There was a crowd of miners and gamblers and reprobates around them, a lot of drinking and backslapping. Somebody discharged his pistol into the floor, and the smell of the powder stunk worse than the miners.

A man stood in the doorway holding his hat upside down and asked Charley for a dollar. The hat was full of paper money. "It's a donation for the greaser," the man said. "On account of the Indian he killed." Charley put a dollar in the hat and moved toward the bar.

Bill was standing next to the Mex, both of them facing Captain Jack Crawford. Charley noticed the Mex was missing half an ear. The gun went off again—Charley saw the smoke this time, it floated up into the ceiling like a departed soul—and then the place went quiet. Captain Jack cleared his throat and opened a copy of the *Black Hills Pioneer,* and began to read out loud. "A Missive to Buffalo Bill Cody," he said, "from Another Old Indian Scout, Captain Jack Crawford. By Captain Jack Crawford."

It took Charley a little while to realize it was a poem.

> *Did I hear the news from Custer?*
> *Well, I reckon I did, old pard.*
> *It came like a streak o' lightning,*
> *And you bet, it hit me hard.*
> *I ain't no hand to blubber,*
> *And the briny ain't run for years,*
> *But chalk me down for a lubber,*
> *If I didn't shed regular tears.*

Charley pried his way through the assembly and got to Bill, who didn't see him. He and the Mex were both fixed on Captain Jack's recital.

> *. . . I served with him in the Army*
> *In the darkest days of the war,*
> *And I reckon, ye know his record,*
> *For he was our guiding star.*
> *And the boys who gathered round him*
> *To charge in the early morn,*
> *War' jest like the brave who perished*
> *With him on the Little Big Horn . . .*

Charley didn't know if he could wait it out. Captain Jack held up his hand for quiet, but there was a demonstration before he could finish. With interruptions, the poem lasted another five minutes, and at the end of it one of the miners drew his pistol and shot the smiling Indian out of the Mex's arm. The Mex was slightly wounded—more burned than shot, but a little of each—so they gave him the money right away, without teasing him.

He accepted it with the same solemnity he'd accepted the poem, and then he turned to the bartender and gave three of the bills to him, and pointed at the empty glass in front of him.

"*Da-me,*" he said. The bartender filled his glass, and then Bill's glass, and then he picked up a glass that was sitting on the bar in front of a sleeping miner, threw what was in it on the floor, and set it in front of Charley. "*Da-me,*" the Mex said, and the bartender filled it too.

Captain Jack refused even before the Mex offered him a drink. "No *da-me,*" he said, more to the room than the Mex, and began another oration. There was something about his voice that nobody else wanted to talk at the same time.

"After the war," he began, "in which my father was killed and I myself was twice wounded, Battle of Spotsylvania, 1864, Forty-Seventh Regiment of Pennsylvania Volunteers, I returned home to New York to find my mother ravaged by sickness. As I wept beside her, she asked one last thing, that I never touch a drop of liquor, and I made that good lady that promise, and it is a promise I mean to keep." To Charley's knowledge, Jack Crawford was the only man in the West who spoke footnotes.

"*Da-me,*" said the Mex, pointing to his glass. And when it was full he turned with it to Captain Jack and offered a toast. "*Tu mama,*" he said, and spilled some of it down the front of Captain Jack's buckskin jacket. Then he drank what was left and turned back to the bartender.

Charley moved closer to Bill. So did the poet-scout. "These are all good men," Captain Jack said to Bill, and pointed around the room. "Miners, paper-collars, even the greaser. But they don't know a thing about Indian fighting. Most of them can't use a side arm at all, except the ones that were in the war, and some of them don't have a stomach for it now."

Bill nodded. The war didn't leave anybody the same. Some of those in it came away too scared to live anymore, and some had spent all the time since looking for excitement to match it. Captain Jack said, "They came here without the protection of the United States government, against the government, into these hills the Indians would claim for their own."

Captain Jack paused and gave the miners and gamblers a chance to agitate against the government. Charley had seen the same sort of thing a couple of times in Kansas, but he couldn't see the point here. There wasn't anybody around to hang.

"And so we have taken up arms to protect ourselves," Captain Jack said, and somebody shot a gun into the ceiling. "Forty-five volunteers, hard-working pilgrims of this territory, ride with me and patrol the mining camps on the outside of town. Three quick shots brings us on the run, and we are never more than a minute from the commencement of action."

Charley said, "Shit, they shoot off side arms in this burg like they used it to keep time." Bill turned and saw him there, and smiled at that.

Captain Jack nodded. "Discipline is always a problem," he said, "in any military situation. Compounded here by the fact that most of the Minutemen have no experience with arms or the military. That is why I would ask you"— he was speaking to Bill now— "to join me as a leader of the Minutemen. Together, we could make Indian fighters of these pilgrims."

"*Da-me,*" said the Mex.

Bill looked at Charley, dead solemn. Charley said, "I already been shot by accident, once in each leg. I know where fate intends to put the third one."

The bartender filled the Mex's glass, and he offered another toast. "*Tu mama,*" he said again.

"No *da-me,*" Captain Jack said. "We're discussing the protection of the miners."

That stopped the Mex cold. He had repossessed the Indian's head and was standing with his foot on one of its ears. As he considered

Captain Jack's words to him, he rolled the head back and forth under his foot, the way a white man might stroke his chin. Finally he seemed to decide on something. He raised his glass toward Captain Jack again and said, "Pro-tess-shion." Then he smiled and killed what was in the glass.

"This greaser wears on you," Captain Jack said to Bill, "but he has proved himself in combat." The Mex set his glass on the bar and picked up the Indian's head. The eyes had shut, like it had seen the bullet coming that shot him out of the Mex's arms.

"*Mis amigos,*" the Mex said. He hugged Captain Jack, then Bill. Then he turned to the rest of the bar and said it again. "*Mis amigos.*" He started out the door, and the miners and reprobates cheered him, and some of them shot their pistols into the ceiling. The Mex smiled and blew them kisses. That caused more shooting and cheering, and the Mex, in a moment Charley considered inspired, stood at the door to the Green Front and blew the room a kiss from his own lips, and then one from the Indian's.

Then he went outside, got on his horse, and drew his pistol. He rode back through town the way he had come in, holding the Indian's head by the hair so it could bounce, shooting his pistol into the air so nobody would miss it. He went out of the badlands into Deadwood proper, where he was arrested by Seth Bullock and escorted out of town.

The citizens of Deadwood did not wring their hands over the workings of the badlands, but they drew the line at being shot in the course of their daily affairs by ambassadors of that part of the city, particularly a greaser carrying a human head.

PERMISSIONS AND ACKNOWLEDGMENTS

"Life in a Gold Rush Town" in *Gold in the Black Hills* by Watson Parker (Norman: University of Oklahoma Press, 1966).

"Deadwood in the Spring of 1877," from a brief dispatch published in May 1877 by the *Chicago Times*. From the collection of the Adams Museum & House, Deadwood.

A Brother's Letter, correspondence from prospector George Robinson to his brother, Stewart. Written January 10, 1878; from the collection of the Adams Museum & House, Deadwood.

"Doomed: The Rise & Fall of Deadwood's Chinatown," by Dustin D. Floyd. Published February 2006 in *Deadwood Magazine*, Deadwood.

Pioneer Days in the Black Hills, by John S. McClintock, an excerpt from the chapter "The Murder of Preacher Smith." ©1939 by McClintock; 2000 by University of Oklahoma Press. Published in 1939 by the University of Oklahoma Press.

"From Sin to Cinders," excerpted from *Gold, Gals, Guns, Guts,* edited by Bob Lee, ©1976, 2004, by the South Dakota State Historical Society Press, www.sdshspress.com. Used with permission.

"Deadwood—A Modern Sodom Needs Another Renovation," by Edward L. Senn, published December 1938 in *Senn's Forum,* from the collection of the Adams Museum & House, Deadwood.

"Wild Bill's Presentiment" in *They Called Him Wild Bill: The Life and Adventures of James Butler Hickok,* by Joseph G. Rosa, originally published in 1964, reprinted and enlarged in 1974, by the University of Oklahoma Press.

"Calamity Jane—With Wild Bill Hickok in Deadwood, 1876" in *Calamity Jane: The Woman and the Legend*, by James D. McLaird, published in 2005 by the University of Oklahoma Press.

"Wild Bill Hickok and His Magic Touch," "That's No Man—That's Calamity Jane," "Jedediah Smith—First White Man in the Black Hills," "Sarah Campbell—First Non-Indian Woman in the Black

Hills," and "Annie Tallent—First White Woman in the Black Hills," in *Tales of the Black Hills*, by Helen Rezatto, published in 1983 by North Plains Press, Aberdeen, SD; used with permission of Midstates Printing, Aberdeen, SD.

"The Mystery Man," an account of Western legend Tom Moore dictated by Deadwood resident Frank B. Bryant, from the collection of the Adams Museum & House, Deadwood.

Old Deadwood Days, by Estelline Bennett, published in 1928 by the University of Nebraska Press, detailing the life of "A Little Girl in Deadwood."

Upstairs Girls: Prostitution in the American West, by Michael Rutter. © 2005 by Michael Rutter. Reprinted with permission of Farcountry Press, Helena, MT. (800) 821-3874, www.farcountrypress.com; exploring the legends known as Madame Moustache and Poker Alice, and providing a list of creative professional names.

Like One Forsaken, the diary entry of W. E. Adams following a family tragedy in 1925, from the collection of the Adams Museum & House, Deadwood.

Deadwood: Stories of the Black Hills, by David Milch/Home Box Office Inc., published in 2006 by Bloomsbury USA, New York, an excerpt from the chapter, "The Color: Gold Makes a Man a Man and Lifts Us Up Above the Baboons."

"Deadwood Mountain," a song written by Big Kenny, John Rich, and Paul Worley, performed by Big & Rich, from the 2004 album, *Horse of a Different Color,* used with permission of Big & Rich, Warner Bros. Records, and Reservoir Media.

The South Dakota Road Guide to Haunted Locations, by Chad Lewis and Terry Fisk, published in 2006 by Unexplained Research LLC, Eau Claire, WI.

Deadwood: A Novel, by Pete Dexter, published in 1986 by Vintage Books, a Division of Random House, New York, used with permission of International Creative Management, New York.

INDEX

A

Adams, W. E., 73, 174–75
Adams House Museum, 32, 129, 134, 174
Anderson, Joseph "White-Eye," 93–94, 96, 97–98, 100, 101
Arnold, Kitty, 96, 99, 100, 101

B

Bartholomew, J. S., 20–21
Bennett, Estelline, 19, 140
Bennett, Judge Granville, 17, 34–35, 140
Big & Rich: Alive in Deadwood (television special), 184
Black Hills
    business census, 1876, 13
    overview, 1–2
    population by place of birth, 6
    population in 1875, 4–5
    population in 1880, 56–57
The Black Hills, Last Hunting Grounds of the Dakotahs (Tallent), 54, 130, 131–32
Black Hills Fair, 70–71
Black Hills Gold Rush and gold, 1–2, 4, 6–7, 12–13, 32–33, 106, 131, 178–83
Black Hills Mining District, 52
Black Hills Trails (Brown and Willard), 52, 64, 117
Brown, Jesse, 52, 64, 117
Bryant, Frank B., 134
Bullock, Seth, 188–93
Bullock Hotel, 187–93
Bully's Bar, 190
Burke, Clinton, 117
Burnham, Alice May, 174

C

Calamity Jane, 21, 79, 88–101, 106, 107, 109, 110–19, 166
Calamity Jane: The Woman and the Legend (McLaird), 88–101
California Joe, 81–82
Campbell, Sarah "Aunt Sally," 113–14, 125–29, 132
Canary, Martha Jane. *See* Calamity Jane
Carbonate Camp, 20
Chicago Times, 23–25
Chinatown, 5, 29–37, 55, 158, 161
Chinese Exclusion Act, 35
Chinese immigrants, 5, 29–37, 55, 158–61, 198
Church, Judge William E., 63
churches and religion, 21–22
Clyman, James, 122–24
Cody, Buffalo Bill, 103, 108, 142
common phrases in Deadwood Gulch, 7–8
Crawford, Captain Jack, 97, 108–9, 204–8
Crook, General George, 114
Crook City, 1
Crow Dog, 61–62
Curtis, William, 126–27, 128
Custer, General George, 104, 113, 127, 128
Custer Expedition of 1874, 113, 125, 126, 128, 132

D

Dakota: A Novel (Dexter), 200–208
dance halls "hurdy-gurdy houses, 16–17, 98–100
Davey, Colonel J. H., 60–61

Dawson, General A. R. Z., 19

Deadwood: Stories of the Black Hills (HBO series), 177–86

Deadwood Bath House, 10–11

Deadwood Gulch. *See* Deadwood

Deadwood Magazine, 29–37

Deadwood Mountain Grand Hotel & Resort, 184

Deadwood Mountain (music album), 184–86

Deadwood mud, 10, 23–24

Dexter, Pete, 81, 200

Dickinson, D. K., 57, 58–59

Dority, Dan, 41–42

Duffield, Frank, 169

DuFran, Dora, 112–13, 115, 116, 119

Duggan, Pat, 60–61

Dumont, Eleanor. *See* Madame Moustache

F

Fireman's Citizen Ticket, 71

fires, 14, 51–56, 65–66, 70

Fisk, Terry, 187

floods, 66–70

Floyd, Dustin D., 29

Fourth of July, 1876, 19

Francis, Charlie, 138–39

French, Eileen, 33, 35, 36

G

Galena, 56, 60–61

Galvin, Seth, 129

gambling houses, 15, 75

Gardner, Captain C. V., 20, 39

Gem Theater, 16, 18, 42, 98

Gilane, James Layton, 64

Gold, Gals, Guns, Guts (Lee, Lindstrom and Lindstrom), 50–71

Gold in the Black Hills (Parker), 4–22

Grand Central Hotel, 9, 19

Green Door (Wild West Winners Casino), 193–95

H

Hallon, Corporal Ross, 65

Harding, J. H., 54

Harris, Moses, 123–24

Harvey, Tom, 64

hauntings, 187–99

Hauser, George, 135–36

Hearst, George, 182–83

Hickok, James Butler. *See* Wild Bill Hickok

Home Box Office, 177

Homestake Hospital, 58

Horse of a Different Color (music album), 184–86

Huckert, George, 171

Hughes, Richard, 96

Hunton, John, 93, 94

I

Ickes, Mrs. Frank, 44

Ivers, Alice. *See* Poker Alice

J

Jenney-Newton Expedition, 113

Jones, Abe, 138

Jones, Smokey, 3, 7–8

Joslin, Lydia Ann, 48

Jules, Simone. *See* Madam Moustache

K

King, John "Casino Jack," 55–56

Kopco, Mary, 32, 35–36

Kuykendall, Judge W. L., 19, 107

L

Langrishe, Jack, 18

Laughlin, W. A., 20

lawyers, 14, 62–64

Lee, Bob, 50
Lewis, Chad, 187
lice and flies, 10–11
Life and Adventures (Canary), 97, 110, 112
Lindstrom, Stan and Wynn, 50
liquor licenses and laws, 73–78
Livingstone, Henrico, 148–49
Low Down on Calamity Jane (DuFran), 112–13
Lull, William B. "New York Billie," 99–100
Lynch, V. P., 64–65

M
Madame Dirty Em, 94, 114
Madame Moustache, 94, 114–15, 163–68
madames and prostitution, 17–18, 114–15, 193–95
Mann, Carl, 82, 84, 86
Mason, Charles, 42
Massie, Captain William R., 82–83, 84, 86
McCall, Jack, 83, 84–86, 107, 110, 116
McClintock, John S., 38–39, 96, 98, 99, 108, 153
McKowan, Z. S., 57, 59
McLaird, James D., 88–89
McShane, Ian, 177
medical facilities and pioneer doctors, 57–59
Melodeon, 18, 22
Merrick, A. W., 20
Milch, David, 177
miners and prospectors, 1–2, 5–9, 11, 19, 33, 59–60
Miss Kitty's Casino, 195–97
Moore, Tom, 134–39
morality in Deadwood, 17–18
Mount Moriah Cemetery, 41, 43, 65, 89, 108, 118, 188, 197–99

My Life on the Plains (Custer), 104

N
names, professional, 173
Nash, Matilda, 203–4
Negroes, 5–6
newspapers, 19–21, 59–60
Nichols, George Ward, 92

O
Old Deadwood Days (Bennett), 19, 140–62

P
Panic of 1873, 32
Parker, Watson, 3, 34, 113
Pioneer Days in the Black Hills (McClintock), 38–49, 108
Pioneer Hook and Ladder Company, 51
Poker Alice, 168–72
Prewitt, Reverend W. E., 44

R
railroads, 142
Rapid City, 1, 9–10
Rezatto, Helen, 102, 121
Rhodes, Jack, 64
Rich, Charles, 84, 87
Richardson, Leander P., 95, 100–101
Robinson, George and Stewart, 26–28
Rosa, Joseph G., 80–81, 89–91, 92
Rosen, Father Peter, 58
Ross, Horatio, 126
Rumney, Reverend W. L., 22
Russel-Collins Party, 130
Rutter, Michael, 163

S

Saloon No. 10, 82–87, 106–7, 110, 178
saloons and liquor, 14–15, 73–74
Schnitzelz Restaurant, 195–96
Schoenfeld, Louis, 42
Senn, Edward L., 48, 72–73
Senn's Forum, 72–78
Seth's Cellar Restaurant, 190
smallpox, 11
Smith, Jedediah, 121–25
Smith, John, 125–26
Smith, Preacher Henry Weston, 21, 38–49, 101
Smith Monument, 43
Sneve, Virginia Driving Hawk, 132
Society of Black Hills Pioneers, 4, 132–33
Solid Six, 71
The South Dakota Road Guide to Haunted Locations (Lewis and Fisk), 187–99
Spencer, "Coal Oil Johnny," 14
St. Edwards Academy, 58
Star, Sol, 34–35
Stokes, George, 9, 98
Swayne's Tar and Sarsaparilla Pills, 11
Swearingen, Al, 16, 98–99, 178, 182
Swill Barrel Jimmy, 12, 144

T

Tales of the Black Hills (Rezatto), 102–19, 121–33
Tallent, Annie, 54, 114, 129–33
Tallent, David and Robert, 130–31
Thatcher, Agnes Lake, 92–93, 104–6, 108

They Called Him Wild Bill: The Life and Adventures of James Butler Hickok (Rosa), 80–87
Thomas, Judge Charles M., 63
Troy, 1
Tubbs, Warren G., 170

U

Upstairs Girls: Prostitution in the American West (Rutter), 163–73
Utter, "Colorado Charlie," 17, 82, 83–84, 92, 93, 97, 106, 107–8, 200–208
Utter, Steve, 93, 94, 97, 106, 107–8

W

Warner, Porter, 20, 55
Wasson, Judge John E., 136–38
Wheeler, Edward, 109, 118
Wild Bill Hickok, 79, 81–87, 92–98, 103–10, 200–208
Wild Bill Hickok: The Prince of the Pistoleers (Wilstach), 89
Willard, A. M., 52, 117
Wilstach, Frank J., 89
Wing Tsue and wife, 35, 160–61
Wolfe, Edmond, 41, 43
Wolff, David, 33, 35, 36, 37
Wong, Fee Lee, 29, 35, 36

Y

Yeomans, Ruth, 48
Young, Harry Sam, 82, 84, 86, 99, 101

Z

Zhu, Liping, 33, 34

ABOUT THE EDITOR

Tom Griffith is a fourth-generation South Dakotan who studied literature and drama at the University of London before graduating with a degree in journalism from the University of Wisconsin–Eau Claire. After working as a reporter, photographer, and managing editor at newspapers in Montana, Arizona, and South Dakota, Griffith helped launch the Mount Rushmore Preservation Fund, a nationwide campaign that raised $25 million to preserve, enhance, and interpret the mountain memorial.

Griffith has written or coauthored fifty books, including The Globe Pequot Press's *Insider's Guide to South Dakota's Black Hills & Badlands* and *Outlaw Tales of South Dakota,* as well as *America's Shrine of Democracy* with a foreword by President Ronald Reagan, *A Winning Tradition* with a foreword by NBC's Tom Brokaw, and *South Dakota,* a comprehensive guide to the state. Griffith's travel features and photography have appeared in numerous magazines and newspapers from New Zealand to New York. A member of the Society of American Travel Writers and Western Writers of America, Griffith lives and writes in the highest reaches of South Dakota's fabled Black Hills.